100 PRAYERS
FOR CELEBRATING
THE LITURGICAL SEASONS

100 PRAYERS
FOR CELEBRATING
THE LITURGICAL SEASONS

Reflections by Leo Piguet

ThomasMore®
– An RCL Company –
Allen, Texas

NIHIL OBSTAT:
Rev. Msgr. Glenn D. Gardner, J.C.D.
Censor Librorum

IMPRIMATUR:
† Most Rev. Charles V. Grahmann
Bishop of Dallas

January 31, 2002

The Nihil Obstat and Imprimatur are official declarations that the material reviewed is free of doctrinal or moral error. No implication is contained therein that those granting the Nihil Obstat and Imprimatur agree with the contents, opinions, or statements expressed.

Acknowledgments
Cover design by Demere Henson
Inside book design by Kim Layton and Becky Ivey

Send all inquiries to:
Thomas More® Publishing
An RCL Company
200 East Bethany Drive
Allen, Texas 75002-3804

Telephone: 800-264-0368 / 972-390-6300
Fax: 800-688-8356 / 972-390-6560

Visit us at: **www.thomasmore.com**
Customer Service E-mail: **cservice@rcl-enterprises.com**

Printed in the United States of America

7484   ISBN 0-88347-484-0

1 2 3 4 5   06 05 04 03 02

Contents

The prayers in this book are taken from *The Faith Connection,* a bulletin insert published by Resources for Christian Living. These 100 prayers were written by a team of writers including Kathleen Dorsey Bellow, Bob Duggan, Carol Gura, Tony Krisak, and George Smiga. They have been adapted for this publication. The accompanying Reflections were composed by Leo Piguet.

Introduction

Leo Piguet was an exceptionally talented man. With enthusiasm he embraced "the spirit" of the Second Vatican Council, a reality that permeated his ministry and his life as a priest. His weekly parish bulletin reflections titled *One Minute for Living* revealed a man of vision anxious to challenge conventional wisdom, but loyal to the Church he loved and believed had been called for by the Great Council. Although I did not always agree with Father Leo's articulations, in my deep respect for him I looked forward each week to his parish bulletin, anxious to be enlightened, amazed, humbled, and at times discomforted by his latest insight.

The publication of his gems was a dream we discussed on a regular basis. I urged him to push forward with the project. Although death intervened, I am delighted that the reflections of Father Leo will now be brought to a wider audience. I believe readers will find a man of passion, insight, and wisdom.

—Most Rev. William L. Higi
Bishop of Lafayette-in-Indiana

> *"Look, the virgin shall conceive
> and bear a son,
> and they shall name him Emmanuel,
> which means, 'God is with us.'"*
> —Matthew 1:23

Advent/ Christmas

What's Your Emmanuel Story?

During Advent we sing "O Come, O Come, Emmanuel." *Emmanuel* is the Hebrew word for "God is with us." Our Advent song is a prayer of yearning for the coming of the Lord in our world to establish his kingdom. Jesus taught us to pray, "Thy kingdom come." Our experience also tells us the kingdom is yet to come, because we do not enjoy harmony, peace, justice, and love all around us.

Our faith, based on experience, also tells us there is more than the "not yet" reality in our lives. We have known Emmanuel moments. One such moment, for example, happened when some parishioners went into the inner city to deliver clothing and food collected by the eighth graders. One home was so cold and dark that it was obviously without electricity and heat. When one of the visitors discovered the situation, he went right to work and got it fixed. That poor family knew God was with them then. And those parishioners will never be the same.

Each of us has our own Emmanuel story. It may be a friendship restored. It might be a person returning to church after some time of alienation. It might have been escaping unharmed after a close call while driving. It might be a prayer answered—a scholarship, a new job, a change of heart.

But the best Emmanuel story isn't told—it's felt. This happens when families come together at Christmas and enjoy each other's companionship and celebrate the experience of God with us.

O Come, O Come, Emmanuel,
    into all the dark and dreary places
        of this world.
O Come, O Come, Emmanuel,
    into hearts that are broken and lives
        that are shattered.
O Come, O Come, Emmanuel,
    into sinful souls—my own included.
O Come, O Come, Emmanuel,
    bring to repentance
        all nations of the world.
O Come, O Come, Emmanuel,
    fulfill your promise of reconciliation.
O Come, O Come, Emmanuel,
    bring your healing love to all.
Amen.

"And the Greatest of These . . ."

In the history of religion as it is recorded in the Bible, it is easy to find two contending forces at work. One force includes those people who are devoted to the Law. The other force consists of those who are more concerned about positive motivation than simple compliance.

Moses told the people to "circumcise your hearts" (Deuteronomy 31:10–16). By that he intended to motivate them to internalize religion so it became more than just external conformity to the Ten Commandments. Moses wanted people to believe in their hearts.

And so did Jesus. Jesus got into serious conflict with the religious authorities of his time—they got him killed—because he tried to lead the people out of legalism into a whole new relationship with God, where God is our Father and we are God's children. We are family.

In a family, obedience and love are both important. In the best of all worlds, obedience flows from love and not from fear of punishment. And the more the love, the less attention to the need for rules.

Perhaps the New Testament writer most committed to preaching the "sons and daughters of God" theme was Saint Paul. In his letters to the Romans and to the Galatians especially, he elaborates his theology of freedom and what Jesus did to liberate us from the bondage of the Law.

It was no accident that Paul decided the greatest of all the virtues is love, and not obedience. How many of us really take Paul's words to heart?

*L*oving God,
how I wish to praise and thank you
for the love you have showered upon me.
God of glory and majesty,
I wish to return your love
and reach out to others with kindness.
Father of us all,
teach me the true meaning of obedience and love,
just as Jesus gave himself over lovingly to you,
in complete and total obedience.
Amen.

Some "Homeless" Have Houses to Live In

Father Henri Nouwen once told the story about how he went to live at Daybreak, a home for persons with disabilities in Canada. One day a woman came to his door at Harvard bringing greetings from the director of Daybreak. He explained that he was busy, that he had classes to teach and meetings to attend; he was sorry but he would have to go. She asked if it would be all right if she just waited for him there. He said it was, but he felt bad that he could not be more hospitable to this stranger.

When he got home, he found his best china out on the dining room table and the aroma of home-cooked food greeting him. The woman had spent the day grocery shopping and preparing an elegant dinner for him. Of course, he ate it with pleasure and was eager to receive her greetings.

The story goes on. He accepted an invitation to visit Daybreak and was not there very long before he was invited to come and live there. Part of the deal included taking care of persons who could not take care of themselves in some of the most primitive ways.

Father Nouwen accepted. He had found a home. No longer was he repulsed by taking care of unattractive people. They had won his love. He would not accept invitations anywhere unless three or four of his Daybreak family accompanied him. He talked about how homeless he had felt before. It gave new meaning to Jesus' words in John's Gospel about his Father's house having many mansions. He nearly wept when he remembered Jesus' words to his apostles that he was going away to prepare a home for them.

*L*et us rejoice and be glad
    for Christ has come
    to show us the path home.
Come, Lord Jesus!
    Bring your light into the
    darkest recesses of the world
    through us, your Body on earth today.
Shed the light of your justice where systems
    oppress the imprisoned,
    impoverish the destitute,
    violate the young and helpless.
Radiate the light of your love where people
    feel abandoned,
    live in violence,
    encounter hatred.
Show us our true home as we address these needs
    in this time and place.
Amen.

The Patron Saint of Control

In Advent we pay attention to John the Baptist because his job was to prepare the way for the coming of Jesus, and the coming of Jesus is what Advent is all about. Take a closer look at the man, at how desperately he struggled for control. He lived in the desert. He ate locusts and wild honey and dressed in camel's hair clothing. He fasted and he prayed. It seems as though it took a great deal of energy for him to control himself.

And how much control did he have over the rest of his life? Even though he attracted crowds and preached repentance with some effectiveness, he had to divert the crowds away from himself and in the direction of Jesus, whose coming it was his job to proclaim. He had to send his disciples to ask Jesus who he was.

Maybe he wasn't even tempted to control his tongue because his mission was to speak out—or rather, cry out—from the wilderness and proclaim the truth. His uncontrolled speech cost him his life when he told Herod's wife what he thought about her marriage and its validity. She knew her husband's weakness for Salome, and there went the Baptist's head.

When you have trouble maintaining some semblance of control over events and people in your life, say a little prayer to John the Baptist. He will understand. He was there, and he kept holy.

All-knowing God,
   you know my inmost thoughts,
   with all my ways you are familiar.
Give me a share of your wisdom,
   show me the truth of my being,
   reveal to me the secrets of my own heart.
May I have the courage to look,
   honestly and deeply,
   at my efforts to control the direction of my life.
Help me to uncover both my strengths and weaknesses,
   to know and follow your will for me
   each and every day of my life.
Amen.

The Baby Jesus

I remember a holy card that a grade-school teacher gave me for getting an "A" in spelling. It was a Nativity scene that pictured Mary kneeling by the baby Jesus and Joseph standing by prayerfully and protectively. The baby Jesus was sitting up in the crib, blessing his mother with the sign of the cross.

At the time, I had no reaction except some pleasure at being affirmed. As I grew older, I began to think about how ridiculous the scene was. Scripture tells us that Jesus was like us in all things except sin, so his agenda as a baby would have been the same as any other baby, then or now: to be warm and dry, to be fed regularly, and to be comforted by the presence of his mother or father.

This didn't last long for Jesus. When he was presented in the Temple, old Simeon picked him up and told Mary that he would be the rise and the downfall of many in Israel, and a sign of contradiction. And she would suffer. When Jesus got lost at the age of twelve and they found him in the Temple, he announced that he was to be about his Father's business. Every child reaches that age when he or she must leave the magic of babyhood behind and begin to pursue his or her life's agenda. For Jesus this was to establish the reign of God, his heavenly Father.

We shortchange Jesus and all children if we stop the Christmas story with a birthday party for Jesus. Pray that each of us makes Jesus' agenda our own: "Thy kingdom come!"

*F*ather God,
>   we praise you for the gift of Mary,
>   mother of your beloved Son,
>   who was wise beyond her years
>   and bore great sufferings in her heart.
Give us faith,
>   that we might follow the example
>   portrayed in the Christmas story
>   of a mother of great patience
>   and an infant son destined to rise
>   from humble beginnings
>   to establish your kingdom among us.
With your Son we pray,
>   "Thy kingdom come!"
Amen.

Welcoming the Prince of Peace

I remember many Christmas seasons impacted by war: the first Christmas after Pearl Harbor, and a few years later the Battle of the Bulge was right at Christmas. It was right around Christmas time, if I recall correctly, that American forces were retreating over the frozen lakes of North Korea. How many Christmas celebrations have been dimmed by the years our sons and daughters were fighting and dying in Vietnam? I forget.

Many of you still remember the euphoria when the Berlin Wall came down and the Cold War began its final thaw. It didn't really last very long, before tribal warfare broke out in several places around the world, the Soviet Union disintegrated, and the stage was set for various types of "ethnic cleansing" in Bosnia and other Eastern countries.

I recall all these situations in these days not to depress anyone, but to remind us of the title Jesus was given in his role as Messiah: the Prince of Peace!

Maybe the big insight to remember from the sad history of Christmases marred by war is to realize that peace will be a gift of God. Peace will come when people will commit to the nonviolent resolution of conflict, to new respect for the lives of all our brothers and sisters, and to the renewed conviction that the Prince of Peace brings what the world cannot deliver.

*L*ights on trees and houses,
Tastes and smells
    that come only once a year,
Smiles and greetings that appear
    on unexpected faces,
Carols floating in the air.
Dear Lord,
    the world around me changes
    this time of year.
We try so hard to surround ourselves
    with comforting sights and sounds.
Help me to remember that,
    with all the beauties of this season,
    the fullest sign of Christmas
    is to make peace with my enemy,
    to include the stranger,
    and to allow others to see
        your love in me.
Amen.

My Favorite Christmas Past

As I think about special Christmases of the past, one jumps out at me. This was the Christmas I spent in an orphanage in 1955 as a chaplain in the Army, in Wiesbaden, Germany. We adopted an orphanage in Assmannshausen, a little village along the Rhine. There were over three hundred children there, and they were all challenged in some way. Earlier in the year, I had found out from the nuns what would serve the institution in the way of gifts. Primarily, they wanted bolts of cloth so they could make their own things, not dolls, not games.

Every payday the sergeant major was there next to the paymaster, begging money for the orphanage from the soldiers. Finally, as we got close to Christmas, we went out and did our buying. We had a truck full of bolts of material, and were eager to see the smiles on the faces of the nuns and the children.

Lots of soldiers wanted to go with us to deliver our gifts. It took two buses to hold them. Upon arrival, we scattered all over the orphanage, because children from various classes had prepared all kinds of skits and musicals for the soldiers. We had a wonderful afternoon.

I went there eager to see the happy looks on the faces of the children and the nuns. And I saw them, all right, but the faces most glowing were those of the soldiers—they received a special gift that year!

*L*ord of history,
    time passes,
    but your love endures.
You have made all things
    and given us a span of years
    to prosper.
Allow us to recognize
    that the time you have given us is holy.
There is no moment
    separated from your power,
    lacking in potential,
    devoid of value.
In each hour we can find
    opportunities to love,
    enemies to forgive,
    strangers to welcome,
    and children to comfort.
Be with us in this moment
    to share the gift or your presence
    and to build your kingdom. Amen.

The Language of Individualism

The language of individualism is "the first language of American life" according to Richard Rohr. "It is a private language of concern, sensitivity, and individual rights. No one in polite company can disagree with it without appearing to be a complete boor. It is warm, affectionate, and infinitely respectful of each person's feelings, hurts, and needs. To be 'politically incorrect' in this area is to incur the wrath of otherwise tolerant liberals and broad-minded believers. Individual rights are the ultimate virtue; individual responsibility is seldom spoken of, lest 'guilt' be incurred" (*Near Occasions of Grace*, Orbis Books).

Playing the victim is an ingenious method of gaining power. No one can criticize you without appearing to be crass and uncaring. You know you're in the midst of such a performance when you hear such phrases as: "You must be true to yourself." "Listen to your feelings." "I have a right to . . ." If you want to see all this in action, just watch the television talk shows.

Father Rohr concludes with some wringing of the hands that our society has used the profound Christian archetype of the Lamb to gain negative power for people who are often merely bitter about their own wounds. Jesus was a victim for us, but his "victimhood" was accepting, forgiving, and never self-serving. The Lamb of God takes away the sin of the world. The victim lambs insist that the rest of the world has sinned against them. The first redeems. The second paralyzes. Let's stop falling for it.

*B*ehold the Lamb of God!
You, who out of love for us
    suffered and died
    that we might live forever.
Behold the Lamb of God!
You, exalted by the Eternal One,
    who will come to destroy
    the evil of this world
    and reconcile all things to God.
Behold the Lamb of God!
You, Lord of past and future,
    who live in the midst of your people
    and feed us with your life.
Give us the courage to build your kingdom.
Strengthen our faith.
Grant us peace.
Amen.

Organizing Those New Year's Resolutions

Maybe one of the reasons New Year's resolutions are so hard to keep is because they are not organized around some familiar and often repeated formula. May I suggest there is such a formula we may have overlooked? It's called the Lord's Prayer. Have you ever noticed when praying the Lord's Prayer that the work is divided between God and us? We ask God in the prayer to "Give us our daily bread, forgive us our sins, lead us not . . . and deliver us." But before we ask God to do anything we pray that God's name will be kept holy, that God's kingdom will come, and that God's will be done. Now who is supposed to do all this? Not God—us!

It makes good sense to put these objectives into resolutions for the New Year. We all know the difference between keeping God's name holy and defiling God's name. We also know if we need to change our language personally to keep God's name holy. When we pray "Thy kingdom come," it's important to remember that God's kingdom is really a state of being, not a place or a new world order. It is best described by adjectives such as peaceful, harmonious, just, loving, gentle, and kindly. We realize that it is not God's job to make the world fit this description—it is ours. What's more, we have the power to make it happen. We determine whether many situations are destructive or life-giving. We can resolve conflicts peacefully. We can make interventions that produce harmony or chaos—it is our choice. We have the power to give compliments, to smile, to be of good cheer. The same is true with "God's will be done . . ." This is our job, to do God's will as we discover it. We know God never wills evil, only good. But God needs us to make good things happen. So consider organizing your resolutions around the Lord's Prayer. Ask yourself, what can I do to keep God's name holy, to make God's kingdom be real in the here and now, and to make God's will be done today?

*O*pen me, O God, to resolve in my heart
to celebrate your name this New Year.
Free me to recognize the enslavement
of my brothers and sisters still today,
in the greed and perversion of those
who exploit children,
in the addictions to power, pleasure,
and profit.
Inspire me to do your will on behalf of the poor,
the exploited, and the alienated.
Restore my soul.
Reclaim my passion.
Recover my potential,
that I might recognize your will
and work with you that your kingdom come
and your holy name be restored once again.
Amen.

God's the Same—We've Changed

When I was already a priest for twenty years, I went to St. Meinrad's Seminary and took a course called "Jewish Studies." One of six Jewish presenters, Rabbi Jochanan Muffs, from Jewish Theological in New York, took us through the Hebrew Scriptures and revealed to us a God I had never before met.

This God possessed human emotions—anger, compassion, vindictiveness, jealousy, and tremendous love. But over and above all this was God's desire for intimacy with humans. Now this is in the Bible and I had read it all along. But I tended to dismiss it because I was aware it meant attributing to God, the pure Spirit, what is human. But of course! How can we relate to a pure spirit? We can only relate to someone like us. This is why the Word of God was made flesh, so we could relate, and thereby make the revelation of Jesus more credible.

I learned that our God wants a deep, passionate, intimate love relationship with God's people. This was not the God who kept score and was committed to justice, punishing offenses and omissions of my childhood, adolescence, and early years in the priesthood. I realized that the God of Abraham, Isaac, Jacob, Mary, Jesus, and our God is not a punishing God, but a reconciling God. Changing one's notion of God helps to change one's notion of self. I know now that I am a sinner, all right, but one who is loved and needed by God. And so are we all.

*B*lessed are you,
    God of our ancestors,
    God of Abraham and Sarah,
    God of Moses and Miriam.
Blessed are you,
    God of covenant promise,
    God of freedom from slavery,
    God of forgiveness from sin,
    God of the Law and the Prophets.
Blessed are you, God of creation,
    for the wondrous way that you have
        revealed your love
    to the children of Abraham, and to me.
May I cherish the roots of my Christian faith,
    sunk deep in the soil of Israel,
    and celebrate your abiding love.
Amen.

God Trusts in Us

Have you ever noticed that engraved on all our coins and printed on all our paper money are the words "In God We Trust"? There is an appropriateness to this motto being on our money—it's okay if Uncle Sam reminds us that we should not place our trust in money. It's as if our leaders had to deal with the question: "What or whom can we trust?" In answering the question by telling us to trust in God, they are right.

But we can ask another question: "Whom does God trust?" The answer is surprising: God trusts people. God trusts us.

One of the marvels that makes God so trustworthy is that God does not give up on us despite our betrayals and infidelities and failures. God made us free and continues to trust us to respond to this freedom by loving God and each other.

God trusts us to proclaim God's presence, mercy, and record of fidelity to the promises God has made in our history. We are trusted to communicate the word and life and love of God in our world, and without us, it simply will not happen.

We pray that we can put our trust in God, not because of the obvious defects of money and things and people to satisfy our ultimate desire, but because God trusts us so much.

In
God
We
Trust

God, Source of all goodness,
Before I can know you or praise you,
    before I can count my blessings
    and thank you for all I have received,
Your Spirit is within me,
    preparing my heart for faith.
Even though I suppose it is my wisdom
    which traces your action
    along the path of my life,
I must proclaim it is you
    who has gifted me with the power to believe.
Allow me to trust you
    and to follow the prompting of your Spirit,
    so that you who have placed trust in me
    might bring it to completion.
Amen.

Epiphany Means Revelation

The first revelation of Jesus to the Gentiles was in the persons of the Magi. They came from the East, following the star, to present gifts to the newborn king. But there were many other revelations related in the Christmas story: the angel to Zachary, the angel to Mary, the angel to Joseph, and the multitude of the heavenly hosts to the shepherds.

The Feast of Epiphany is special to us because we come from the Gentiles, too. Most of our family roots are not Jewish, but Teutonic or Celtic. So we identify with the Magi as people who were latecomers to salvation history, just as we are. Even though our spiritual roots are Semitic, giving us a kinship with Abraham, Isaac, and Jacob, our family heritage is Gentile. We celebrate the fulfillment of the prophecy of Simeon, who chanted at the Presentation of Jesus in the Temple: ". . . a light of revelation for the Gentiles, and the glory of your people Israel."

Each of us might respond to the feast we celebrate today by asking how God continues to reveal Jesus in our daily lives. Certainly through the presence of God in the Scriptures and the sacraments, but where else?

May I suggest that we look in the faces of the poor, the starving, the oppressed, and those suffering from mental illness, alcoholism, and various addictions. Jesus comes to us wearing many masks. It would be a shame to miss him because all we see is ugliness or need. When he comes to us in beauty, we celebrate. When he comes to us in misery, can we accept the challenge?

*L*oving God,
    in your Son, Jesus Christ,
    you have offered all people,
    and me included,
    the gift of salvation.
Thank you for showing me the way to Jesus
    through the Catholic Church,
    my spiritual home.
Thank you for the grace of the sacraments,
    for the way you have revealed yourself
        to all nations,
    and for the Church, which unites us
        to our spiritual heritage.
May I always be eager to share
    these wonderful gifts with others,
    and may I never look down on others
    as less worthy of your grace,
        or forsaken by your love.
Amen.

Scared Stiff

Isn't it funny how our colloquialisms can serve up the truth so honestly? Fear can stiffen the limbs and the heart so we can't even act. We know what it's like to be scared stiff. And sometimes that's okay. Fear keeps us from stepping in front of speeding cars, entering the interstate without looking, or jumping in water over our heads when we can't swim. Fear can be life-saving.

But there must be something about fear that Jesus doesn't like. I never counted the times he said, "Fear not" or "Do not be afraid" or "Do not let your hearts be troubled," but it was often.

Did you ever wonder why?

Maybe it's because fear can immobilize us to the point of being dysfunctional. And Jesus wants us to be doers of the Word, not just hearers only. To be a doer one must act, and sometimes it takes courage. Courage means dealing with a difficulty instead of withdrawing from it.

What can arouse courage?

Maybe another fear. Shakespeare wrote: "Our doubts are traitors, and make us lose the good we oft might win, by fearing to attempt" (*Measure for Measure,* I, iii, 78).

Perhaps love, too. Saint John said: "Love drives out fear." Let us pray for the kind of trust which comes from love of God and frees us from destructive fear.

*J*esus,
> time and again, I have asked you,
> "Teach me your ways, show me your will."
Yet, when you bid me
> to abandon everything for you,
> I am afraid.
Counting the cost is not the way
> of your follower.
Open my frightened heart
> to commit my life to you,
> without reserve,
> once again.
Renew my weary soul
> with a new passion for your kingdom
> and a trusting attachment to you,
> my Savior and companion.
Amen.

Jewels for Stones for Jewels

It seems there was a couple growing old in a small town. They had raised a large family and worked hard for a living. But they had a problem. Everywhere they went they had to carry around a large sack of stones. Stones of all kinds: field stones, granite chunks, bricks, and concrete. They picked them up along life's way, from the family, from friends, from work, and even from church.

The stones were a collection of painful memories, unhealed wounds, senseless slights, and unforgiving anger—a very heavy burden to carry.

One day, there was a handsome young man in the town square, exchanging jewels for stones. They hurried to the square to make an exchange. The woman was hesitant, but with some fear handed over her whole sack of stones. The young man gave her a little change purse. She opened it and found diamonds and rubies and other precious gems. The load was so light, and she was so joyful.

Her husband, on the other hand, was not so quick to make a deal. He took out each stone and dealt each stone away one by one. The young man never grew impatient. Finally, the husband had his precious gems and headed home happy.

When they were gone, the handsome young man smiled, turned and began to crush each stone. From each one he extracted a precious jewel, which he put in a little purse to make himself ready for the next exchange.

What did Jesus mean when he said, "My yoke is sweet and my burden light"?

God of all ages,
    your love for us spans the breadth of life.
You are Lord of both the young and old,
        the weak and strong,
        your faithful followers,
        and those who seek to believe.
Embrace us in your love,
        encircle us with your care,
        ease the burdens of our lives
            with the jewels of your love.
Let us know the value that you place upon us,
        that it is not our circumstances,
        but your presence that gives life.
As long as we live, both here and hereafter,
        we are all special in your eyes.
Amen.

Tough Goals, Flexible Plans

Our lives are much more self-directed when our goals are clear. Goals represent a desired future state, and usually are hard to accomplish in less than five years. For instance, ridding the world of hunger or illiteracy—just can't do those things overnight. Goals need to be not only clear, but cherished, so they would not be abandoned when inevitable obstacles are encountered.

Plans, however, are different. Sometimes called objectives, plans are a description of results we want soon, such as: I want to collect this definite amount of money to send to Catholic Relief Services for the hungry in Ethiopia by the end of the month.

But plans need to be flexible. Too many things can happen, too many things beyond our control. It snows. Whoops, where did that cold sore come from? Darn, lost in the mail. He missed the plane? Grandma is sick; we can't go on vacation now. That movie played for the last time yesterday. Didn't you know this restaurant is closed on Monday?

Father Henri Nouwen once wrote about how his ministry kept being messed up by interruptions. It seems he was very attached to his ministerial plans. Then he realized his ministry was the interruptions.

James and John, sons of Zebedee, most likely saw their life plans as being good fishermen, just like their father. In that simple society, sons normally followed the same career as their father. But Jesus made them change their plans one day when he strolled by and invited them to "Come, follow me." Good thing their plans were flexible.

*L*ord Jesus,
 you called James and his brother John
 to follow you and to be your disciples.
So, too, in ancient times,
 the Lord called Samuel to serve God's people.
Help me, Lord Jesus,
 to listen carefully for the sound of your call.
I know that you love me,
 that you speak to me in many
 and various ways.
May I always recognize your voice
 and know that it is you,
 and no ordinary interruption.
May I always respond faithfully,
 as did James and John and the other disciples,
 "Speak, Lord, your servant is listening."
Amen.

The Importance of Praying
for the Sick, with the Sick

To pray for and with the sick is important because very often people who are ill are unable to pray by themselves. Maybe they are in a lot of pain. Pain can be very distracting and demand all one's attention. Sometimes trauma leaves one a little woozy, and it's hard to make sense of words and thoughts. Sometimes pain medication adds to the confusion.

I prayed a lot once during a personal surgery experience, but it was not the kind of prayer one would offer publicly. Thank God for the Hail Mary. Thank God for the memory of those ritual prayers. Little memory is required. One of my constant companions was, "I know that my redeemer lives." Another was Handel's consoling melody and sometimes Scott Soper's.

We Catholics are sometimes shy when it comes to praying with the sick. The only visitor I had during that hospitalization who offered to pray with me was a Protestant minister friend. I don't think I was conscious at the time of my need for someone to pray with me.

A friend who went through similar surgery confided in me that he wanted to pray in the worst way. He decided to pray the Lord's Prayer, but could not find the words. They just would not come back to him. Maybe the desire to pray is an elegant form of prayer in itself. I often tell sick people their prayers are very valuable and encourage them to pray for various intentions. To pray in the midst of obstacles to prayer, God knows, only adds to the value of the prayer.

*L*ord Jesus,
>   you showed your love and compassion
>   by the many miracles of healing
>   that you worked.
I know that you care for and watch over
>   all who are sick and who suffer so terribly.
Help them, dear Jesus,
>   to feel your healing love.
Console those
>   for whom a physical cure
>   is not to be forthcoming.
Strengthen their faith
>   and the faith of all who care for them.
Lord Jesus, help me, too,
>   so that I will be strong of faith as well.
Amen.

Have You Been Jesus to Anyone Lately?

When we remember the revelation of Jesus to the wise men from the East, we look for times when Jesus has revealed himself to us in our own time and lives. We believe Jesus does continue to reveal himself in all times. Usually, however, this surprising appearance of Jesus does not come through some private revelation where Jesus talks to us.

To be Jesus to someone means that we have given a person an experience of the presence of Jesus in our world today. I believe Jesus counts on us to do this for each other. When Jesus walked the earth, he taught, healed, forgave, prayed with, prayed for, challenged, tricked, accepted, suffered, worked patiently, and sometimes condemned. But everything he did and said came from a heart brimming over with love.

Let me list a couple ways I feel people have been Jesus to me. Perhaps at the top of the list is the comment one person made to me when I was objecting to someone else's solution to a problem. He said, "We'll deal with your ego in a minute." It reminded me of Jesus saying to the apostles when a pagan had impressed him, "I have not seen such faith in Israel." Some humor, truth, some shame.

Jesus comes to me through the mail each year at Christmas. Personal notes of support and affection are moments of acceptance, like those Jesus gave to so many people who were imperfect. To those who have made me feel the presence of the Lord, I give you my gratitude. And I hope I have been Jesus to somebody, too.

*J*esus:
Some of us have experienced
    deep moments of your presence
    but have had little time to distill their meaning.
Some of us have for so long followed
    the routine of daily service
    that it is difficult to remember
    when your Spirit has last touched our hearts.
As we come together in Christian community,
    let our strengths and weaknesses interact.
Let the energy of those elated by your love
    rouse the faith of those who have forgotten the vision.
Let the wisdom of those who have borne
    the trials and blessings of a lifetime
    provide a foundation for those who are new.
Together let us be Jesus to each other.
Amen.

"The time is fulfilled,
and the kingdom of God
has come near;
repent, and believe
in the good news."
—Mark 1:15

Lent

The Temptations of Jesus and Our Addictions

On the first Sunday of Lent we are reminded of the temptations of Jesus at the end of his forty-day fast in the desert, just before he began his public ministry.

First the devil tried to manipulate the hunger of Jesus into an exercise of power: "Command these stones to become loaves of bread" (Matthew 4:4). Then he tried to capitalize on Jesus' self-esteem. You are really somebody. God won't let anything happen to you. "He will command his angels . . . they will bear you up" (Matthew 4:6). The third temptation had to do with worldly riches. After showing Jesus all the kingdoms of the world in their magnificence, the devil said: "All these I will give you, if . . ." (Matthew 4:9).

Jesus knew what it was like to be tempted as we are tempted. He was hungry. Bread was so attractive he could almost smell it. And he had the power! Power, the need to be in control—how much we want this! It is one of our addictions. The next temptation had to do with prestige, another of our addictions. You're really somebody! How much we want people to think of us that way. Finally, Jesus overcame the temptation to possessions. The devil offered an alluring vision, but Jesus saw that he could not have these things and God at the same time. Sometimes we think if we have the right possessions, we will have prestige and power.

Perhaps during Lent, we can look for symptoms of these addictions to power, prestige, and possessions, and begin practicing their antidotes— prayer, fasting, and almsgiving.

*J*esus, my Healer,
I require your power in my times of need.
I depend upon you
    for strength and hope.
So often I become paralyzed by my pride
    and crippled by my addictions.
Although I need you more than ever,
    I lose my power to turn to you
      when my possessions and self-importance
        detract me from you.
Make me thankful this day
    for those in my life who stand by me,
    for those whose example and love
      give me strength,
        and carry me to you.
Amen.

Subtle Temptations

Father Richard Rohr, O.F.M., claims that temptations to pornography and blasphemy and grand larceny are very easy to recognize. It's the more subtle temptations that will get us if we don't watch out. These temptations seem to be reserved for people who are used to abundance. They are not the temptations of the poor. He is convinced that the poor and the affluent are both in need of liberation, but the rich are held in bondage by different oppressors. The poor are oppressed by outside forces, the rich by forces inside themselves—namely, attachment to their own opinions and feelings.

Here is Father Rohr's explanation of the meaning of the temptations of Jesus. The temptation to turn stones into bread is the temptation to have our work be effective. If we work, we want to see the reward of our work. The devil wanted Jesus to play games with God by throwing himself down, remembering that God promised the angels would bear him up. Father Rohr claims this is the temptation to be right. And finally, there is the temptation to fall down and adore the kingdoms of this world. Maybe this is a little easier to see as a temptation—for Father Rohr it's the temptation to be in control.

Now it is no sin to be effective, to be right, and to be in control. But it is the need for these things that can become addictive and therefore occasions of sin. Let us pray that we may move toward some degree of detachment from our own opinions and feelings and our need to produce, to be right, and to have control.

God, you are the Holy One,
    and you call me to avoid sin.
You have shown me the path of life
    and asked me to follow it.
How often I am tempted to fall short!
How often I feed my own selfishness
    and turn a deaf ear to your truth!
Help me to understand that
    even in my weakness
    you accept me as your child.
Even when I am tempted toward selfishness
    you claim me as your own.
Even when I am tempted to let go
    of my responsibilities to you,
    you refuse to let go of me.
Amen.

"Love Your Enemies." Are You Serious, Lord?

I don't think I know anyone who has not felt falsely accused or unjustly treated by someone. When this happens, it's normal for us to want that person to pay for it. How right it feels for them to hurt just as they made us hurt. In our imagination we celebrate the triumph of justice over injustice as we make pictures of their misfortune.

In the midst of these fantasies which make us feel so justified, we don't like to hear words like these: "Be holy, for I, the Lord, your God, am holy. . . . You shall not bear hatred for your brother in your heart . . . take no revenge . . . cherish no grudge. . . . You shall love your neighbor as yourself. I am the Lord" (Leviticus 19:1, 2, 17, 18). And Jesus takes the law of love even further: "Love your enemies . . . pray for your persecutors" (Matthew 5:44).

What is this? Just as we identify those awful people who hurt us, and imagine all those appropriate punishments, we hear Jesus tell us: "Good work! Now you know who the people are that you most need to love and pray for!" This is downright unnatural. How on earth do we deal with it? When Jesus said pray for them, he knew that people with any semblance of a conscience can't pray to a God who has forgiven them so much and still ask God to do bad things to others.

Want to make a big step toward holiness? Imagine the face of an enemy. Imagine a smile coming over that face as something good happens. Enjoy the moment. The big step you made was from your own heart into the heart of God.

Dear Lord,
　　you know the weakness
　　of our human condition.
It is so difficult to love
　　when we have been hurt.
It takes such strength to forgive
　　when we have been disappointed.
It requires such courage to trust again
　　when a relationship has been betrayed.
Let us remember your humility
　　when you became one of our race.
Teach us to forgive those who have failed us,
　　not to dismiss them from their negligence
　　but to forgive them with kindnesses.
Amen.

Remove a Cross a Day

Normally when we think of being a disciple of the Lord, we realize that it means bearing crosses. Jesus told the apostles that if they wanted to be his disciples they must be willing to take up the cross daily in order to follow him. And by the real cross he carried on our behalf, Jesus showed he wasn't asking us to do something he wasn't willing to do himself. In fact, he spent a lot of time removing crosses from people.

He removed the cross of hunger from the five thousand with loaves and fishes; he took the cross of guilt from the paralytic and then the cross of paralysis; the cross of an issue of blood from the suddenly bold woman on the road; the cross of grief from Jairus and Martha and Mary; and the cross of addiction from Mary Magdalene. We could go on and on and discover the bulk of Jesus' ministry was taking crosses away.

In many much less dramatic but just as real ways, we can remove crosses from people every day. Here are some suggestions: Hold that complaint. Speak to a stranger. Smile at your child. Reserve that judgment. Congratulate an achiever. Encourage an underachiever. Smile at the police. Wave at that farmer on the tractor. Compliment your spouse. Bring a sack of staples for the food pantry. Smile at a cashier. Say "yes" when asked to volunteer. You complete the list.

It's amazing how much lighter one's own cross becomes each time we take one off someone else.

Blessed are you, God of the Universe,
   for you grant us every good thing.
Through your grace,
      we pray that we might pay heed
         to the crosses of others,
               giving food to the hungry,
               sharing our resources with the poor,
               offering support and compassion
                  to the grieving,
               refusing to give in to the powerful grip
                  of hatred and prejudice.
Refresh us with hope
      and transform us with your love
      that we might bear our crosses
         and lighten those of others in your name.
Amen.

Resentment Reeks

Ivan and John were farmers. Their fields adjoined. Something happened once that made Ivan very hostile toward John. Ivan was filled with a kind of resentment that he carried with him constantly. He dreamed about ways he could hurt John.

One day, the Lord appeared to Ivan. The Lord wanted to help deliver him from his grudge. So the Lord offered Ivan anything he wanted in this world, but with the provision that the Lord would give John twice as much as Ivan asked for.

Well, Ivan had to think this offer over. So he slept on it.

The next day Ivan told the Lord he had decided what he wanted. "Blind me in one eye," he told the Lord.

No matter how justified we might feel, a grudge has an unescapable result—some kind of self-destruction.

Feelings of resentment create grudges. To hold a grudge is to keep oneself in a kind of bondage. To let a grudge go is always a victory for freedom.

Jesus forgave his executioners because when he commended his Spirit into the hands of the Father, he did so out of pure love—he did not want it to reek of resentment.

He wanted it to be holy, so it would not foul the Father's hands.

*G*od of compassion,
    you alone know the depth of my pain.
You are aware of the people I have loved,
    but who refused to love me in return.
You were with me when those I trusted
    betrayed my faith in them.
Only you can understand
    how words and actions
    have left me wounded and alone.
Heal me of my hurt.
Allow me to break those chains of pain
    that bind me to my offenders.
Through your strength, show me
    how to forgive,
    how to move forward,
    how to live.
Amen.

Beyond Consumerism, What?

One of the most countercultural institutions in our religion is the season of Lent. Our culture says: "You deserve a break today." But Lent says: "You deserve a penance today." Lent calls us to transcend the material and treasure the spiritual. This is countercultural.

One of the strongest features of our culture is consumerism. Of itself it isn't a bad thing. The vitality of our economy depends on people buying and selling products. Research efforts attract billions of dollars to produce better products for us, the consumers. Having a vibrant economy produces jobs and enhances the quality of life, sometimes even our spiritual lives.

But there is a hazard. It's called the "consumer mentality." And it threatens our spiritual health. Everything becomes a product, even people. I remember a prospective bridegroom who insisted that his fiancee undergo a complete examination by a doctor, a psychiatrist, and his family before he would set a wedding date. Of course, he would not submit to these tests himself. They did not get married; the bride was wise enough to know products wear out or get obsolete.

All of us have some radical selfishness to deal with, and it is this instinct the consumer mentality serves. A committed consumer has only one standard of judgment: Does it serve me? A committed consumer is only a buyer, never a giver. Lent calls us to hear the invitation of the Lord to be producers of the kingdom of God by giving people love and joy and peace. We learn to move from a consumer to a producer by exercising. And these exercises are prayer, fasting, and almsgiving.

God of life,
    we find ourselves in the desert
    of our own selfishness
    as we struggle to choose you.
During this season of Lent
    we long to seek union with you in prayer,
    to empty ourselves in fasting,
    to make room for your graced presence,
    to give generously of our time, talents,
        and resources to those in need.
Grace us with the power of your Spirit
    to live these lenten resolutions,
    to turn our lives around,
    to unite ourselves to one another in love for you.
Amen.

The Supreme Sacrifice

Eight-year-old Johnny was very serious when the doctor called him into his office at the hospital and explained how he could save his little sister's life. Mary, age six, was near death. Her only chance was a blood transfusion. Since the two children had the same rare blood type, Johnny would be the ideal donor.

"Johnny," he asked, "would you like to give your blood for Mary?"

Johnny hesitated a moment, his lower lip trembling. Then he smiled and said, "Sure, Dr. Morris. I'll give my blood for my sister."

The operating room was prepared and the children wheeled in— Mary, pale and thin, Johnny, robust and almost cherubic. Neither spoke, but when their eyes met, Johnny grinned broadly.

As Johnny's blood siphoned into Mary's veins, her pale skin began to turn pink. There was complete silence as the operation proceeded. But then Johnny spoke in a brave little voice the doctor said he will never forget. "Say, Dr. Morris," he said, "when do I die?"

It was only then that the doctor realized what that moment's hesitation, that almost imperceptible trembling of the lip, had meant when he had talked to Johnny in his office. He thought that giving up his blood for his sister meant giving up his life! In that brief moment he had made his great decision. Johnny probably could not tell us that Jesus said, "The greatest love a person can have for his friends is to give his life for them" (John 15:13). He lived it instead.

*H*oly, holy, holy Lord!
In Jesus Christ, you have chosen us
    in our weakness and sin
    to be the beneficiaries of your life
        of love and sacrifice.
Let the trust that you have in us
    be a source of grace and blessing
        to deepen our spirit of discipleship,
        to be courageous on the way of the cross,
        and to journey faithfully
            until we reach our home with you.
Let heaven and earth be filled with your glory
    forever and ever.
Amen.

What Gives You Life?

What gives me life? What enriches me from my ministry as a priest? From the time I was a very young priest and went to the home of a family who lost a two-year-old child from pneumonia, I have been impressed with people's faith. I went there to console this young couple, and they consoled me. As much as we are confronted with death and the grief it brings, almost always those who are survivors inspire me and give me life by their faith.

Some of the most life-giving moments occur in the midst of something liturgical. To say, "Lift up your hearts!" and hear the people respond, "We lift them up to the Lord!" is a thrill for me. To see the born-again look on the face of an adult who has been through the catechumenate, who comes out of the waters of Baptism and throws his arms around me in a grateful embrace is hard to match for its life-giving power.

To be involved in the reconciliation of an inactive Catholic is a peak experience, especially when he or she displays surprise and joy at how easy it is. To be involved in the reconciliation of a couple whose marriage is fragile is so rewarding. Preparing young couples for marriage is always a hope-filled time because they offer such promise for healthy family life. To move them to think beyond the ceremony to the covenant is exciting. The wedding is a day, but the marriage is forever.

I am grateful to all who have made my life worthwhile.

*B*lessed are you, faithful God,
　　for in Jesus you have revealed
　　your unconditional love for us.
Blessed are you, God of covenant love,
　　for in the blood of Jesus you have shown
　　how lovers are willing to suffer
　　for their beloved.
Blessed are you, God of life,
　　who invite us into the mystery
　　of your own divine, creative love.
Blessed are you, God of presence,
　　for you enrich us with the many examples
　　of people who bear witness in their lives
　　　　to your divine love.
Amen.

We Are Called to Be Forgiving

The God of Abraham and Jesus is unlike other gods. Our God is filled with a forgiving spirit.

Anyone who accepts this God as his or her own God has a special call, therefore, to be forgiving.

Forgiveness isn't easy, because the times we are most in need of offering forgiveness are the very times we feel most like withholding it, because we feel so offended, abused, and violated.

We tend to wait for an apology before forgiving, and even though an apology may be appropriate, what if it doesn't come? What if the person by whom we feel offended feels totally innocent? An apology will never come, and we are left to carry around the heavy load of an unforgiving spirit.

Could it be that the one who feels guilty of an offense is called to apologize and the one who feels offended is called to forgiveness? It may be this simple.

Help me, Lord, to develop a forgiving spirit, and, like you, love enough to accept apologies when they are given, but not demand them when they are not.

*L*ord Jesus,
    help me to be compassionate
    as you have taught.
May I refrain from judging others,
    and may I always seek to find
    the good in their lives.
Gentle Healer,
    you came to bind up our wounds,
    to take our brokenness
        into your loving embrace.
Grant that I may be an agent of your healing love.
Let me touch others with your forgiveness,
    your mercy, and your unconditional love.
Amen.

Sin Is Its Own Punishment

In the Hebrew Scriptures we find God making initiatives with the people, such as creation and covenants. Usually the people respond to God's initiatives with enthusiasm. But it often wears off as the strain of relationships and the allure of secular attractions take their toll.

The people either forget God, or they choose something other than God as their highest value, or they actually rebel. In other words, they sin.

God has to get their attention all over again, and sometimes it must feel like punishment. Sin is often its own punishment.

At any rate, the story goes on. People repent and do penance. God rescues them and they are once again reconciled. Over and over again, the original enthusiasm, coupled with gratitude for the rescue, returns. And then the process starts all over again as the enthusiasm wanes.

God initiates.
People respond with enthusiasm.
People forget and sin, feel punished, repent, and are rescued.
Joy returns—for awhile.

I suspect we have all experienced this dynamic in our spiritual journey. I wonder at what chapter in the story each of us has reached right now.

*L*ord Jesus,
   help me to understand
   the terrible reality of your sufferings.
Help me to appreciate
   how empty your soul must have felt
   when you cried out,
   asking your Father why he had abandoned you
   in your time of desolation.
Show me that my own times
   of sadness and abandonment
   are filled with the hidden presence
   of your Father's love.
Help me once again to be obedient
   to the will of the Father,
   to accept in love
   whatever comes my way,
   and to offer all my sufferings in union with yours.
Amen.

Lent: A Time for Change

On the Sundays of Lent we sing our response, "Create in me a clean heart" (Psalm 51:10). These are the words of the repentant psalmist. From a heart that is sullied with sin, we ask deliverance. This prayer is not quite so radical as the God of Ezekiel who says: "I shall give you a new heart" (Ezekiel 36:26), as if God saw the old heart had no chance of being healed.

If we are with Lent, we are far beyond thinking about little lenten resolutions, like giving up candy or alcohol or desserts. If we are with Lent, we are agonizing about how difficult it is to walk through life trying to transform our consciousness. For a Christian, the transformation of consciousness means nothing else than following the imperative of Paul to the Philippians: "Have this mind in you which was in Christ Jesus!" (Philippians 2:5)

Make judgments with the mind of Christ. Have you ever wondered how different our judgments might be if we did that all the time? This mind of Jesus has us doing good to those who hate us, walking an extra mile, not seeking the repayment of debt, and letting those who have offended us get away with it. If we are thinking with the mind of Christ, we are not devising ways of punishing or getting even, but ways to forgive and be reconciled. How much have I used my imagination lately to figure out ways of doing good to those who have harmed me? If the answer is never, then we know how far we have to go to think with the mind of Jesus.

*C*hrist, our light,
　　we are all blind sinners.
Come with your vision,
　　your insights,
　　your perceptions,
　　and heal our darkness.
As we prepare to celebrate the mystery
　　of your dying and rising,
　　heal our shortsightedness.
Reconcile us to those we have judged;
　　turn our very lives around.
May you dwell in our hearts and awaken us
　　to follow you more deliberately.
In the power of your Spirit we pray.
Amen.

The Greatest Christian Feeling

When Paul listed for the Corinthians the top virtues of the Christian—faith, hope, and charity—he told them the greatest of these is charity, or love.

Going through Lent and Easter brings a number of feelings to a practicing Christian, such as sorrow for sin during Lent, a sense of grief on Good Friday, and real joy on Easter. Thinking about what must be the greatest of Christian feelings, I cast my vote for gratitude. Lent and Easter remind us of what God has done for us in Jesus Christ. Through no merit of ours, which means we couldn't earn it if we wanted to, God has taken away our sins and given us the promise of eternal life. Pure gift. Amazing grace.

What feeling could possibly be more fundamental for a Christian than gratitude? This may explain why in Third World countries, where people don't have phones or inside plumbing, or two sets of underwear, and have to wonder what they might eat tomorrow, they are filled with the joy of the Gospel. It's their gratitude.

Every time we celebrate the Mass we are primarily making an act of gratitude. This is what *eucharistic* means. Just listen during the eucharistic prayer for references to gratitude.

When we feel grateful, we want to say nice things to people, like "Thank you." Often, when we feel gratitude we want to show it by sending a note or giving a gift or doing something in return. Gratitude is the basis for nothing but good words and actions. Can you think of this feeling ever leading to something bad?

*B*lessed be you, O God, Creator of the cosmos,
  for you have loved me into being,
    filling me with goodness,
    making me a temple of your Spirit.
With a grateful heart I desire
  to know and love you more fully
    through faithful observance
    of holy rest in you!
May the season of Lent take on a new meaning for me
  as a time of deepening my communion with you,
    with my brothers and sisters in the human family,
    and with the web of life that is your creation.
Amen.

Jesus: Victor over Self

It's 4:45 A.M. and I'm asleep in a guest room of the house of some friends. I hear what sounds like the blast of a diesel locomotive right outside the door and realize in a second it's the alarm system. After a few seconds, the alarm stops blasting and I have to make a decision. Do I stay put, or do I go see what's up and run the risk in the darkness of being mistaken for a burglar?

I did not want to get shot on my vacation, so I stayed put. Sure enough, they had put the dogs out without disarming the system first. We laughed about it later.

And what does all this have to do with Easter?

Holy Week and Easter lay before us both the realized potential of human beings for violence and the ultimate triumph of nonviolence. In the Risen Lord we see the victory of good over evil, life over death. But there is a personal victory that also needs to be highlighted. It is the victory of Jesus over self. It happened in the garden when he prayed that the cup might pass, that there might be another way, but then submitted to the will of his Father.

Our culture tells us that when we have a want it becomes our right, and anyone who stands in the way does us an injustice. This is immature, of course, and burglars are distorted examples—they take what they want with no regard to rights. But we can all look at Jesus' dying to self, and realize such dying is the key to everlasting life.

*H*oly God,
  I praise you and bless your name!
Just as Abraham, our father in faith,
    obeyed you,
    so may I always seek to do only your will.
Just as Jesus was obedient unto death,
    even death on a cross,
    so may I always be faithful to your call.
Just as Jesus became a blessing for all humankind,
    so may my life bring good to this world
    and be a blessing for others.
Amen.

Loving God Back: What's in It for Me?

In the Bible, God initiates activity. God creates, gives orders, rewards, punishes, makes covenants, promises, keeps promises, and saves the people. "God has first loved us," John proclaims (1 John 4:19). In many ways, the Bible is an elaborate invitation for the people to love God back. For God to be a tremendous lover is one thing, but there is no love affair unless we love God back.

God's mighty deeds speak convincingly of God's love. Rescue after rescue, despite the sinfulness of the people, the agape quality of God's love for us is revealed. Agape means to love without hope of return. Selflessly. Loving God creates a relationship of friendship with God, which no one-sided love arrangement can produce. Saint Augustine told people: "Love God and do as you will." Loving God is the great secret of liberation. When we love God and do as we please, we never are overcome by sin. We may fail, but sin will not prevail because it contradicts our heart's desire, which is to love God back.

In our culture we have been conditioned to ask: "What's in it for me to love God back?" as we do for any and all investments we might want to make. To ask such a question hardly seems irreverent or blasphemous. So I'll stop. I'll resist the temptation. I suggest that, maybe if we follow Jesus on his journey of love to death and resurrection, we will want to seek such agape, such a capacity to love without hope of return. And not because of what's in it for us, but simply because we are grateful.

*L*oving God,
   thank you for the gift of love
   that you have poured out on us so lavishly.
In the face of my sin
   and the countless sins of others just like me
   your relentless response
   has always been the same.
Time and time again,
   you have forgiven
   your sinful children
Even when we refuse your love,
   and betray your covenant,
   you never cease to forgive and forget.
Help me to grow in horror at the reality of sin,
   and never let me stray far from your embrace.
Amen.

Passiontide

Jesus began his "passion" when he was born. The experience of coming into human life introduced him to such primal sufferings as being cold and hungry and wet.

Being like us in all things except sin, he probably knew the terror of wondering if his mother had left him when she didn't immediately answer his cry or handed him to someone else. He knew the need to be comforted when he skinned his knee or bumped his head.

Immersed in the human condition, he shared our fears and our joys. Even as an adult, he was known to shed tears. He did not live his human life with a compromised humanity.

He knows what it's like to be us.

It's important for us to realize how human Jesus was. When we hear the stories of the passion during Holy Week, we are hearing about a human being in agony. Even to the point of sweating blood, which is further than most of us ever have to go.

Theologians tell us that Jesus could have redeemed us without going through so much suffering. One of the big mysteries to me is why he had to go so far. Maybe it's us. Are we so hard to convince we are loved that Jesus had to go to such a horrific death to prove it?

Perhaps one of our big challenges as we remember the passion of Jesus is to believe so strongly in God's love for us that Jesus will know it was all worthwhile.

Jesus, my Redeemer,
I believe that I have been saved
    through your passion and cross.
I acknowledge that the gift of eternal life
    is nothing that I have earned
    or can deserve.
As I reflect upon the suffering of your passion,
    let me center on your love
    and my unworthiness.
Humble me to remember the times
    that I fail to defend the innocent
    and cooperate with evil.
Lead me to claim my own responsibility
    for your crucifixion
    and to resist the temptation
    to blame others.
Amen.

It Felt So Good to Pray

For a long time I judged the quality of my prayers by how they made me feel. If they made me feel good, I considered them to be prayers of high quality. That was a long time ago. Since then I have learned a little more about prayer, because I've learned a little more about life. Pleasure and excellence, when equated, can produce illusion.

When a parent gets up in the middle of the night to quiet a crying child, it may not be much fun, but it's quality parenting.

When a lover accepts the negative feelings of the beloved, and remains present in compassion, even though it's miserable for both of them, it may not be much fun, but it's quality loving.

When an employer treats a deficient employee with humanity, and tries to move the person gently toward better performance, it's not a barrel of fun, but it's quality leadership.

When a child does his or her chores without a long face, and without delay or nagging, it gives no pleasure, but it's quality obedience.

When prayer makes us feel good, it's time to be suspect about the quality of our prayer. Besides, it's really God's job to evaluate the prayer, not ours. I suspect that when the prayer is most dissatisfying to us, it may please God most. At least, when we don't feel like praying, and we persevere in prayer anyway, we know we're not doing it for ourselves, but for God. That's quality prayer.

*L*oving God,
   as the first disciples asked Jesus how to pray,
So I ask you
   to teach me to worship as I ought.
May I always have a keen sense of being part
   of a "holy communion" of prayer,
      together with all the saints
         and angels of heaven.
May I rejoice to be part of your chosen people,
   eager to praise and worship you,
      eager to join with others in celebrating
         your divine mysteries,
         in the sacred liturgy of the Church.
Amen.

We Never Stop Growing Up

One Sunday, while driving the short distance from the parish house to the school we used for Mass while our church was being built, I picked up a few minutes of a religious program on the radio. I heard a priest who had just returned from a sabbatical discuss all the reading he had done during that leisurely time. What struck him most from all his reading was an author who wrote something like this:

"We know a child has become an adolescent when he or she becomes self-conscious. We know an adolescent has become an adult when he or she begins to notice others and cares about their needs. One reaches Christian maturity when one makes a personal commitment of service to others."

Life seems to be—from this formula—a kind of "arsis" and "thesis" revolving around self. When self is foremost in our attention, our maturity is compromised.

To deny one's self during Lent, therefore, is an exercise of growth in maturity. But it's only a first step. The second step is to reach out lovingly to others, to be willing to make sacrifices to meet their needs.

Let's not give up on the fifteen- or sixteen-year-olds, who may be mostly conscious of themselves these days. They may well have their own feast day sometime.

O God of perfect love,
    we thank you for the saving cross
        of your Son, Jesus,
    who died that we might live.
Give us courage this Holy Week to die to sin,
    sacrificing self—self-reliance, self-righteousness,
        self-doubt, self-importance, self-hatred.
Help us to love like Jesus,
    to pour ourselves out generously like a libation
    to show such example
        that others may know and love you.
Humble our stony hearts;
    let everything we say and do profess
    that Jesus Christ is Lord,
    to your glory and praise.
Amen.

Let's Hear the Whole Story

Some scriptural images are very consoling, but they can also be deceiving. Take the Good Shepherd image, for instance. The Good Shepherd spends his time thinking of the sheep and making sure they are safe. When we think of Jesus as our Good Shepherd, we are comforted because Jesus protects us, and keeps us safe; Jesus pursues us when we stray and rescues us from all danger, including our sin; Jesus saves us and is the loving giver—we are the happy receivers.

Many of us become so attached to Jesus who does all these good things for us that we think that's what our religion is all about, receiving good things. One of everybody's favorite hymns ("On Eagle's Wings" by Michael Joncas) says it poetically and so well: "And he will raise you up on eagle's wings, bear you on the breath of dawn, make you to shine like the sun, and hold you in the palm of his hand."

In a consumer-driven society like ours, a religion that offers all this care taking would be "hot." But it is not Christianity. Christianity makes demands as well. A case could be made in fact that Jesus does all these wonderful things for us so that we would be free to do what he wants of us. He wants us to love each other as he has loved us. His one law is not that we let him shepherd us, but that we love each other, in fact that our giving and receiving get so mixed up that it's hard to tell the difference.

*Help Me
Reach Out
to Others*

*L*oving Shepherd of my soul,
    I thank you
    for your constant protection
    and for the way you guide my life.
Jesus, my Savior,
    you are the Good Shepherd,
    you have given up your life that I might live.
Help me to reach out to others
    with the same selfless love
    that you have shown to me.
Help me to embrace as sister and brother
    all who are different from me,
    all with whom I may disagree,
    all who are in need of your love.
Amen.

"Do not be afraid;
I know that you are looking
for Jesus who was crucified.
He is not here;
for he has been raised,
as he said."
—Matthew 28:5–6

Easter

The Radical Call of Easter

For forty days we prepare for our annual remembrance of those events in the last days of Jesus' life that produced our salvation. For three days we immerse ourselves in the story. Then it takes us fifty days to get over it! Welcome to Eastertide! Shed whatever compromises the joy that pervades this season because Christ has overcome death for himself and for us! Paul sums it up like this: "Be intent on things above rather than things on earth. After all, you have died! Your life is hidden now with Christ in God. When Christ our life appears, then you shall appear with him, in glory" (Colossians 3:2–4).

Such is the radical effect of our baptism. It couples us with the death and burial and resurrection of Jesus in a real and mysterious way. We become new creatures. We are grafted onto the body of Christ, reconciled, reborn, renewed, restored to a state of innocence, and promised a share in the inheritance of God's obedient Son.

The Hebrew people experienced God's mighty deeds in their behalf for generations, and they survived on the promise of the coming of the Anointed One. To express their feelings of joy and thanks and praise they created a word that we have discovered also expresses our sentiments precisely. It is *Alleluia!* "Praise the Lord!"

But it doesn't mean a thing unless it expresses some real feeling of gratitude to God for Jesus, for all our gifts, and for the hope of eternal life. May we join our "alleluias" in a testimony of faith, hope, and charity during every Easter season!

*G*lorious and eternal God,
   we bless you this Easter season
   for the saving sacrifice
      of your dearly beloved Son
   who died willingly on a cross
      that we might live.
Through his resurrection,
   may we live
      truly convinced of your love
   and committed to your peace.
By the holy power of the Spirit,
   make us so strong in faith
   that through our daily lives
   others too may come to believe.
For Christ is risen! Alleluia!
Amen.

Living Out the Paschal Mystery

More than once I have heard preachers talk about the calling of Christians to live out the Paschal Mystery of Jesus Christ in their own lives. Let me try to explain what this means. For Jesus it meant living through the Good Friday, Holy Saturday, and Easter experience: suffering, dying, lying in the tomb, and rising. For us it means abiding the sad endings we experience in our lives, enduring the awkward in-between times, and working for new beginnings.

It is not unusual for people with good jobs to become unemployed, for example. Companies are merged; people have to go. Or a corporate decision dictates that a high salaried executive is expendable. It happens all the time.

The person terminated has a sudden Good Friday experience. To feel victimized and angry about it is normal. To let it go is not easy. But unless one is liberated from all these negative feelings, it's hard to begin the agonizing search that must happen if there is to be a new beginning. For the unemployed, getting a new job is the Easter experience.

Paul writes that we have to make up in our own bodies what is lacking in the sufferings of Christ. What is lacking is not on the part of Christ, but on our part. We make up for what is lacking when we join our sufferings and risings with those of Jesus and thereby feel at one with him in his sorrow and in his joy.

*H*eavenly Father,
    you gave your Son to be born,
        to suffer, and to die in this world;
    we give you praise
        for this redeeming act of love.
In the passages of our own experiences
    of endings, sufferings, and new beginnings,
        unite our pain to the passion of Jesus.
Fill us with the hope of resurrection,
    and the faith to believe
        that we will be united with you
            in rejoicing,
        through Jesus our Savior.
Amen.

Living Out the Paschal Mystery, Part Two

Witnessing adult baptism by immersion is a thrilling experience. These people emerge from the water actually looking reborn, as they are: "Do you not know that all of us who have been baptized into Christ Jesus were baptized into his death? Therefore we have been buried with him by baptism into death, so that, just as Christ was raised from the dead by the glory of the Father, so we too might walk in newness of life. For if we have been united with him in a death like his we will certainly be united with him in a resurrection like his" (Romans 6:3–5).

In Baptism we are identified with Christ in the mysteries of our redemption. We die with Christ; we are buried with him; we rise to new life, which is God's life in us. Good Friday, Holy Saturday, Easter Sunday—this is the heart of the "Paschal Mystery."

So we identify with Christ not only at Baptism, but all through our lives. Good Fridays and Easters keep coming. If we accept these realities as they come, we live out the Paschal Mystery of Jesus. And how do we do this? Jesus gave us the touchstone: "Love one another as I have loved you!" Often it is simply a kind word, a restraint from scolding, a compliment. "Loving is being willing to make a sacrifice to meet the genuine need of another."

May Easter move all of us to identify with Christ all through the year.

*T*hrough the waters of Baptism
    unite us to the Paschal Mystery
    of Jesus' saving life.
Through the waters of Baptism
    embrace us as your daughters and sons
    and join us to the body of Christ.
Through the waters of Baptism
    draw us into the welcoming arms of your Church
    and beckon us into the sacramental life.
Through the waters of Baptism
    let your Spirit fall upon us all
    and let us renew the face of the earth.
Amen.

"To Jesus Heart All Burning"

Luke's Gospel about the two disciples on the road to Emmaus gets me thinking about hearts that burn. They said to each other as they reflected on their experience: "Did not our hearts burn within us as he talked to us on the road?" (Luke 24:32). It made me think of the hymn "To Jesus Heart All Burning." It is a consoling thought to have the heart of Jesus burn when he thinks of his love for us men and women. We have all probably known what it is like to have our hearts burn over something, or for someone. But beware of burning hearts!

Burning hearts can make you dissatisfied with the ordinary. We have to live out our spiritual lives in the ordinary day-to-day existence we all know. Now and then it is spiced with a spiritual thrill, but this is always a kind of consolation, not the regular fare.

Burning hearts do not of themselves make you holy. Burning hearts are more like the sizzle than the steak. When prayer is filled with fantastic consolations and lots of tears and feelings of intimacy with God, we can be deceived. Prayer without such effects but continued with perseverance is always more trustworthy. We know we're doing it for God and not for ourselves.

Burning hearts are everywhere, and often make little sense. In Brighton, England, thirteen people were hospitalized and hundreds were treated for hysteria and hyperventilation trying to get into a concert by the latest American pop group.

I still like to think of the heart of Jesus burning with love for us— with all our strangeness.

*L*ord Jesus,
>like the disciples on the way to Emmaus,
>>I often journey in confusion and disbelief,
>>acting as if you were gone forever from my sight.
>Help me, Lord Jesus,
>>to recognize you
>>>in those who journey with me along the way,
>>to recognize your presence
>>>in the Word of Scripture,
>>to deepen my love for you
>>>in the breaking of the bread.
>May I always know and experience
>>your presence in my life.
>Amen.

"We Believe in the Resurrection of the Body"

We often hear questions about the resurrection of the body. Questions such as "How old will my body be?" "Will physical imperfections still show in the glorified body?" "What about a body that was cremated?" These questions, the late retreat master Father George Maloney, S.J., asserted, are ridiculous because we already live in a resurrected body!

To be a Christian means to live out the Paschal Mystery of Jesus, his death, burial, and resurrection. We have been united with him through faith and Baptism, and therefore we have been coupled with his death and burial and resurrection. Being one with the Risen Christ, we are also risen. What death does is free us from the obstacles the human condition places in the way of realizing what we already have. Death allows us to see the reality of our risen condition by taking away all that limits our vision in our present state.

This is why the saints often welcomed death. Their faith had already taken them beyond death in their unity with the Lord.

What a consolation it is to realize that those close to us who have died are still the same persons, but are now united with the Risen Christ, fully human, fully aware of God's presence, fully alive, sharing the promised inheritance of God's own Son. This kind of faith made Paul exclaim: "O death, where is your victory? O death, where is your sting?"

*G*iver of life,
  in the death of Jesus,
  you reveal the Risen Christ.
In the life of your disciples,
  you speak a proclamation of faith.
Renew within us the promise of Baptism.
Immerse us in the saving life of Jesus,
  that, against relentless destruction,
  against disdain for the value
    and beauty of life,
  your living Word will prevail,
    over and over again.
Amen.

Bodies Are Important

"I believe in the resurrection of the body." We believe that our body will share in the destiny of our soul. Like Jesus' body after his resurrection, however, it will have different properties. We call it a glorified body. But it will be a real body, our body.

In many ways, this is a very sensible teaching. Think of all the good things we could never do if we didn't have a body. We could never give anyone a smile. No one would ever see a look of compassion in our eyes and be comforted. No one could ever get a hug or give one. And think of all the bad things we could never do if we didn't have a body. We couldn't stick out our tongue at anybody, or bop someone in the nose. There would be no rape, no armed robbery, no shootings. We can fantasize sins in our minds, but we can't act them out without a body.

So it makes sense for the body to share in the ultimate destiny of the soul. But there are some down-to-earth realities about bodies we need to notice. For instance, experts tell us that less than 10 percent of communication happens through our choice of words. Our tone of voice and facial expressions account for 90 percent. So if we are looking to improve our spiritual life, we might take the body seriously and give special attention to one of its parts, our tongue: "If a person never makes a mistake in what he says, he is perfect, and is able to control his whole being" (James 3:2).

*C*hrist, my Savior,
    in quiet moments I have meditated
    upon your sufferings during the passion.
I have ached as I envisioned your body
    beaten by whips and scourges,
    crushed by the weight of your cross.
I have imagined that if I had been there with you,
    I would have acted to relieve your pain.
Allow me to see that your body in the world
    today is still broken by the divisions
        among your disciples.
If today I would give you comfort,
    lead me to respect all those
        who believe in you
    in all my words and actions.
Amen.

Easter Is an Attitude

I was talking with a dear friend about an episode that happened between us maybe a year prior. We were both quite angry with each other at the time. We both probably yelled some angry words. Funny thing, neither of us could remember what the issue was.

I suspect that if it had been some sort of good thing that happened between us, and that we had celebrated instead of fought, we would remember. Isn't it remarkable that it's so easy to remember good things that bring us joy and celebration, and so hard to remember bad things that cause conflict?

The best thing that ever happened in this world we remember at Easter. Jesus rose from the dead and proved the truth of his words, giving us confidence in the way he keeps promises, giving us the experience of new birth and the expectation of life eternal. As C. S. Lewis wrote in a book called *Surprised by Joy,* faith in the resurrection of Jesus can give us an attitude of joy so securely based that we do not lose it even in moments of tragedy. Abiding joy is the attitude of an Easter person. Luke wrote his Gospel with an Easter attitude. Even as he relates the horrors that were part of Jesus' life, there is a pervading conviction about the reality of ultimate triumph.

To see how real Easter is in the lives of people when they are confronted with death or terminal illness is truly inspiring. Jesus overcame death by his resurrection. This is the good thing we can never forget. It makes joy possible even in the midst of misery.

O God, I believe
   that you are the first and the last,
   the one who lives, and is present
   to your people through the gift
   and power of the Holy Spirit.
I believe that the grace of Jesus' resurrection
   continues on for all ages,
   in the wonder of forgiveness,
   as you draw all together in your embrace
   of reconciling love and joy.
I believe that you are acting every day
   in the human family,
   inspiring us to overcome our conflicts
   and abiding with us in our celebrations.
Amen.

Admire the Women

As we read the Easter accounts in the Gospels, notice how well the women stayed together. Even though they wept and felt deep sorrow at the death of Jesus, they did not come apart like the men. They went to the tomb to minister to the body with the customary treatments given to the dead. They were the first to see the empty tomb and the first to believe in the resurrection. They were the first to proclaim that Christ is risen.

On the other hand, the men are weak and full of skepticism and attribute the women's proclamations to histrionics. They were scattered and disorganized. They went into hiding filled with fear and probably a lot of remorse. After all, one of their number had betrayed Jesus and committed suicide in apparent despair. Peter, their leader, had denied Jesus three times. All the rest had abandoned him when he needed them most.

For the men, his presence once again was just too good to be true. Too good for such unworthy disciples, they must have thought. But when Jesus spoke to them, it was not with words of condemnation, but simple words of peace: "Peace be with you!" (John 20:19) Easter was a time to purge away the self-pity and shame, to feel forgiven, to realize that God does not hold their sins against them, to accept the spiritual healing of this powerful affirmation and start getting serious about doing what God needs them to do.

So as we go through another Easter season, admire the women of the Gospel stories and be inspired by the men who rise to Jesus' call of discipleship.

God the Father,
>with the Son and the Spirit,
>you brought about the salvation of the world,
>which we celebrate this Easter season.

Today especially, we thank you
>for the gift of women who labor in love,
>making sure that the necessary things of life
>>get done with grace.

In them we know your motherly concern for the world.
Inspired by their example, we learn
>that brothers and sisters must love one another
>and work together for the good of the family.

Bless our mothers;
>keep them always close in your life-giving love.
Amen.

Relations and Reconciliation

We live in a world of relationships. We have to relate in so many ways with so many forces. With nature we relate differently when it's warm and sunny from when it's cold and snowing. We relate with the people in our lives every day. Some of these are pleasant relationships; some can be stormy. We also relate to our own selves, and when we have a cold or some inner grief, it's harder than when we feel happy and healthy.

Often we forget, but we also relate to God all the time. God sustains us with the gifts of life and air and grace. When we feel needy, we relate to God in prayer; sometimes we even remember to be grateful for God's presence and goodness.

Now is a good time to think about how much control we have as individuals over the quality of many of these relationships. When we experience harmony with nature, with others, with ourselves and God, we have true peace. When there is disharmony, we sometimes admit—in moments of honesty—personal responsibility. We see ways that we could change and make things better. As we think about our relationships, we grow closer to the whole process of repentance; we feel sorry about the way we have acted and determined to do better.

From very early on, religious people have felt a need to be assured of their goodness and God's forgiveness. Jesus forgave our sins and continues this reassuring ministry in the Church through the sacrament of Reconciliation. Try it sometime. Feel the healing power of forgiveness and affirmation.

*M*ay your light shine upon us,
    O Risen Lord!
In that dazzling light, open our hearts
    to be transformed in love.
Take our selfishness
    and spark in us a fire for justice.
Take our prideful quest for power
    and ignite a new passion for the poor.
Take our angry, vengeful hearts
    and radiate in us a new spirit
    of repentance and forgiveness.
Take our mind and spirit and soul,
    creating us anew,
    that we might offer in return
        a witness to your saving graces
        that spill out over this world.
Amen.

Free Will Is God's Gift

In a poem entitled "Freedom" by Charles Peguy, God wrestles with the realities of human freedom and its risks. They may not always choose the best thing. They may even harm themselves and others. God finally decides that freedom is a precious gift because without it men and women could not choose to love. "A beatitude of slaves, a salvation of slaves, a slavish beatitude, how do you expect me to be interested in that kind of thing? Does one care to be loved by slaves? . . . Once you have known what it is to be loved freely, submission no longer has any taste."

At Easter we celebrate the choice God made to redeem us by sending Jesus, who chose freely to be the victim whose blood would wash away our sins. So we would not miss the point of his life, Jesus said: "The greatest love a person can have for his friends is to give his life for them" (John 15:13). Notice the direction. The greatest love is always for others, not for self.

To give up one's own life for the sake of others we call "the supreme sacrifice." On Good Friday, Jesus made his. To give up one's own life is one thing. It is a choice made in freedom. To take another's life is quite another thing, especially if the life is taken in behalf of one's own freedom. The same God who gave us free will and so cherishes our freedom also gave us the Ten Commandments, and one of them forbids taking human life.

To cherish human freedom is not the same as applauding human choices. Our God does not applaud death-dealing choices. Our God forbids them.

*L*ord Jesus,
>   on the night before you gave your life for us
>   you prayed that we all might be one.
We have not followed that command.
Those of us who believe in you
>   have separated ourselves from each other
>   and cemented our differences into walls.
We cannot proclaim your good news with one voice
>   because we do not respect the freedom
>   that belongs to us all equally.
Lead us to mourn our divisions and heal our wounds.
Show us how to respect life,
>   our life and the life of all others.
Amen.

Mary, the Chief Disciple of the Lord

During the months of May and October we give special honor to Mary. Pope Paul VI added to her many titles when he called her the "chief disciple of the Lord." This title tells us about the quality of her faith and makes her a powerful model for us. Some of the things she had to deal with make our problems seem much smaller.

"I'm going to have a baby and I'm not married." What could she say to Joseph? Nothing. She had to depend on God—for whom nothing is impossible—to save her, and that's where she put her faith.

"Jesus is lost, Joseph. We must find him." For three days they searched, with hearts filled with anxiety. To be entrusted with the Savior of the world and to lose him makes for deep feelings of desperation.

"My son is making enemies. He is in great trouble." How could her gentle son be so confrontational toward the authorities? They have so much power and he will not fight. How he trusts the Father!

"My son is dead." Now my faith in the Father must be stronger than ever.

"My son is risen!"

*M*ary, woman of compassion and strength,
   overshadow me with your mantle of love.
Bearer of God,
     open me to bear Christ to the world,
     nurturing my restless spirit and hungry soul.
Woman of poverty and oppression,
     transform me in the spirit of the *Magnificat*
     that I might see injustice
     and act to lift up the lowly.
Woman of sorrows,
     join my suffering to that of your Son
     and the sword that pierced his heart
     in that one great act of redemption.
Mother of humanity,
      gather your people in a song of glory to God.
Amen.

How Does the Holy Spirit Work?

Here's an interesting thought: The Holy Spirit did not come upon the apostles and disciples until they had a chance to pray together for nine days, to experience the need for divine assistance, to grow in love and respect for each other, perhaps even to effect some reconciliation among themselves. After all, not only did one of them betray the Lord, some of their number denied and deserted him. They had to get beyond such guilt. The Holy Spirit came upon them when they had become church enough for the Holy Spirit to dwell therein.

We all know how hard it is to be church. Many of us have our little private relationship with God or Jesus, or maybe even the Holy Spirit, and don't give much personal attention to being community. Can we fend off the pressures of our culture all by ourselves and care enough about each other to produce the other-centered atmosphere "church" implies? Or does it take the presence of the Holy Spirit to draw us out of self and into loving concern for all God's sons and daughters? Do we have to somehow invite the Spirit into our lives and be open to the conversion the Holy Spirit has historically brought about?

However we answer these questions, waiting until we are church enough or working to make church happen, our role is clear. Our role is to become Spirit-inspired Christians. We have one law: "Love one another, as I have loved you." If we do this, we will know the Holy Spirit is in our midst. We will make each other feel the presence.

O Divine Spirit,
    pour forth your gifts
    upon your Church.
Just as the good Pope John prayed for
        and gave his life for the gift of unity,
    so may I seek always
        to strengthen the bonds of love
        among all followers of Jesus.
By a kind of new Pentecost,
    renew your gift of unity in our time.
Remove the barriers that still divide us;
    heal the wounds that separate us.
May we be one as you are one,
    forever and ever.
Amen.

Discovering the Presence of God

If you don't discover God in your daily lives, you won't discover God at all. Do you discover God on retreat? In the mountains? At the beach? In the foxhole? Most of us aren't in these places very often, so we're in trouble if that's only where we find God. In my own experience, discovering God is something like Christopher Columbus discovering America. When he did it, he didn't know what he had done. Only later did he realize what he had found.

Most of us experience God more as past event than present. We look back and suddenly understand God was there with us but we were not aware at the time. Maybe it was a dramatic moment, such as a close shave in an automobile. Maybe it was a tender moment with a person who was sick, a reconciliation with a friend, or the breathless beginning of a romantic liaison. Looking back, we are sure God was there shaping the event, somehow protecting us or giving us a precious gift.

For many people, God's presence has been dramatic and life-changing. Many Christians who call themselves "born again" testify that they can point to a specific moment in time when God was present to them and they gave themselves to the Lord. This has not been my experience. God seems close to me at some liturgies and also during moments of private prayer. I also count on my "sacramental imagination" to help me discover God's presence. I look at the host and the cup and experience a comforting reality of God with us. Where do you discover God present?

God of all truth,
I know I have seen your presence
    in the beauty of a scarlet sunset,
    in the power of a thunderstorm,
    in the yellow sweep of a summer meadow.
I recognize that you are there
    when I serve the poor,
    when I choose the good,
    when I protect the weak.
I can sense your closeness
    in the love of my family,
    in the touch of a child,
    in the compassion of a friend.
Help me also to see your love
    in the faith of another person,
    even when that faith differs from my own.
Amen.

Listening in a "Pious Coma"

Frank Sheed—street preacher, writer, and publisher, and a very active Catholic layman in his time—talked about how we sometimes listen to the Scriptures at Mass in a "pious coma." We hear very powerful words but they are so familiar to us they have no impact.

Being aware of this "pious coma" idea, I listen to the Scriptures with more attention and would like to share a couple wide-awake reactions with you. Never before when we read the passage of John's Gospel where Jesus gave us his law of love: ". . . that you love one another. Just as I have loved you, you should love one another." (John 13:34), did I make a connection with the words he spoke just one sentence before: "My children, I am not going to be with you much longer" (John 13:33). Jesus connected his going away with our need to love each other as he had loved us: You be me to one another while I'm gone.

On the Feast of Saint Mark, we hear from the letter of Peter: "Disciple yourselves, keep alert. Like a roaring lion your adversary the devil prowls around, looking for someone to devour" (1 Peter 5:8). I wonder if that roaring lion might be the other side of the "love one another as I have loved you" coin. Just as we play the role of Jesus in the life of another by our love, do we not also play the devil when we do not love? Today we pray that we can love one another according to the standard Jesus set for us, that we can discern the prophets from the devils, and keep our Easter joy all year.

*F*ather, awaken us from our pious coma
    that we may love as you have so loved us:
  "I ask not only on behalf of these,
      but also on behalf of those who will believe in me
        through their word that they may all be one.
As you, Father, are in me, and I am in you,
    may they also be [one] in us,
    so that the world may believe that you have sent me.
The glory that you have given me
    I have given them, so that they may be one,
      as we are one,
    I in them and you in me,
    that they may become completely one,
    so that the world may know that you have sent me,
      and have loved them even as you have loved me."
(John 17:20–23)

Easter

*"The time is fulfilled,
and the kingdom of God
has come near;
repent, and believe
in the good news."*
—Mark 1:15

Ordinary Time

"Follow Me" and Be Surprised

In Scripture anyone who receives a call from God and says "yes" runs into surprises, and they are usually disturbing. Read the story of Mary, the mother of Jesus, as the prime example. But not everyone is as full of complaints as the prophet Jeremiah who cries out, "You have duped me, O Lord." Can you imagine a holy man scolding God? Sometimes God does the scolding. When Peter tries to talk Jesus out of going down to Jerusalem where his life would be in danger, Jesus tells him, "Get behind me, Satan!"

Imagine the apostles before Jesus came into their lives. They had a fairly clear vision of what their careers would be like. In that culture, to know what life will be like as an adult, all one had to do was to take a look at one's parents or grandparents. Changing careers was not popular and to some extent not even possible.

The apostles had quite comfortable notions about religion too. Keep the Law of Moses, obey the commandments of God, and say the prescribed prayers. Someday the Messiah will come, drive out the Romans, restore the sovereignty of Israel, and establish the kingdom of peace and harmony among the chosen people. In the case of the apostles, there must have been more than a superficial spirituality at work. They must have had a yearning for more than external observance in their religious life. Look how they responded when Jesus said to them, "Follow me." Then look at what happened to their attitudes and their careers and their lives. Look at how they handled surprises.

*I*n Christ's return to your right hand,
    O God of our dreams and longings,
       you reveal to us our future.
Keep your promise bright in our hearts,
    that we might journey in this life
       with a longing that rouses us
    to be faithful witnesses of the Gospel,
       and with a desire that wakens us
    to the gift of your abiding presence
    and overcomes all surprises.
As you lead us home,
       keep us sure-footed on the path
    which reveals your holy reign,
       both now and forever.
Amen.

Confrontation, Never Fun

How good are you at confrontation? In a family situation, it happens all the time. Whenever children are corrected, it happens. When children are "talking back," it happens. Those in work situations often encounter confrontations with fellow employees, bosses, and even customers. I am terrible at confrontation. I turn into a wimp at the thought of it.

In a letter I found from a dear friend, Dr. Charles Riker, while doing my annual desk clearing one year, he wrote: "If a person is not good at confrontation, he might consider the following. When he confronts the second person there will be negative emotion. This condition implies lack of forgiveness. So what if he tried a different tack? The different tack: During a meditative moment, examine oneself for lack of forgiveness in the direction of the other's imperfections. Take whatever steps are familiar for thinking of forgiveness and reconciliation if that person were not the one to be confronted."

He concluded by writing that he didn't know why this works, "but who knows how electricity works?" Perhaps if we look at the hazards of confrontation without prior forgiveness, his advice seems even more sane and possible. Who wants bitterness? Worse. Who wants to carry around an unforgiving spirit? It's much too heavy a load. Let it go.

*L*ord Jesus Christ, you are
   "the Way and the Truth and the Life."
Show me how to love
   all of my sisters and brothers,
   not merely in speech,
      but in deed, in fact, and in truth.
Teach me how to be humble
   about my own grasp of the truth,
   to listen and to learn
      from the truth that others share.
Give me the gift of understanding,
   that I might handle confrontations
   with a forgiving spirit.
Amen.

Prayer as Political Activity

Have you ever thought of prayer as political activity? Part of the political process includes compromise, deal making, and lots of persuasion. We use these same techniques in our prayers. We try to persuade God to make something happen our way. Sometimes we give God a deal it seems tough for God to refuse, such as giving up cigarettes if our prayers are answered.

Sometime we use prayers to manipulate or condemn people. We hear them at times when the general intercessions are spontaneous. For instance, at a charismatic Mass where the bishop was presiding, someone prayed: "That the bishops will be open to the Holy Spirit, we pray to the Lord." The implication could be that this person felt the bishops were closed to the Holy Spirit. I suspect the bishops feel they aren't closed. I don't know if our bishop resented that prayer or not.

Of course in the Psalms we find prayers of vindictiveness. Some Psalms are violent, asking God to make enemies sterile or impotent or worse. These are the prayers of people in trouble, and it's hard to feel gentle and patient when you're under fire.

Whenever we pray for people to be different, perhaps pray they become a lot more like us, we are engaging in political prayer. And you know what? God accepts all our prayers without irritation. God takes our prayers, even when they may rise from a bitter heart, purifies them, and is pleased we prayed. Good thing God isn't just like us.

*C*ome, Holy Spirit,
   fill your people with love and fervor
      for the Gospel.
Come, Holy Spirit,
   heal the Church of whatever
      would cause scandal or disillusionment.
Strengthen our faith
   that the power of your divine love
      may dwell within us.
Empowered by your presence,
   may the example of my faithful life
      give witness to your saving presence.
Amen.

Can Churches Be Truly Hospitable?

In his book *The Company of Strangers,* Parker Palmer deals with the question of how the Church can ever be truly hospitable. He asserts: "The essence of hospitality—and of the public life—is that we let our differences, our mutual strangeness, be as they are, while still acknowledging the unity that lies beneath them" (p. 130). Palmer argues that openness to the stranger and letting the stranger be is resisted by the basic dynamics of community formation. An intimate community is formed by an act of exclusion: "We" are in and "they" are out. To have a sense of community suggests that we have drawn a boundary around ourselves and that we see ourselves as different from the surrounding world. The stranger can threaten the very foundation of such a community by blurring the boundary. Therefore, the stranger must either be kept out or made to become like us.

But Palmer offers a solution. "When a community's identity is rooted in the truth that we are all members of one another—that our deepest identity is in our commonality in God—then it can embrace the stranger with grace and ease" (p. 131). His own experience fortified this when he worked in a soup kitchen in New York. He found it a place of hospitality where he felt the unity which ran beneath the vast and tragic differences between him and the clients who came for soup.

Practice the presence of God and listen to our voices change. From division to healing; from self-protection to vulnerability; from criticism to compliment.

Jesus, you welcomed the stranger,
>> the despised, the foreigner, the sinner
>> into your compassionate
>>> and healing love.
> Free my cluttered heart
>> that I might truly follow
>>> your way of welcome.
> Open me to look into the eyes
>>> of the poor and the lonely
>> to sit with the troubled and grieving,
>> to listen to sinner and saint alike,
>> as I yield to your spirit of welcoming.
> Amen.

A Modest Suggestion

All of us know what it's like to be in conflict with another person. Often it is a person we love and who loves us back. If the conflict goes on for a while, it can turn into a kind of trench warfare with long moments of silence and sudden bursts of attacking and defending.

And through it all, feelings of sadness, hostility, anger, vindictiveness, and self-pity assail us. These feelings hurt, and it's tough to get our attention off of self. In the meantime, the relationship deteriorates and a kind of sullen fog blocks out the sunshine

There is a way to break out of this without intensive counseling. Try giving the one with whom you are in conflict a genuine compliment now and then. No big deal, just a simple, "Say, your hair looks nice today." Or maybe, "I like the way you handled that situation with George yesterday." Or, "You really are good with children."

Just the attention it takes to come up with a compliment that's true, simple, and not a big production (that arouses suspicion) might be enough to distract oneself from one's feelings long enough to reach out to the other in kindness. And it might be catching. It's hard to be in conflict with someone who appreciates you.

Blessed are you, God of mercy,
    for the countless times
    that you have forgiven me.
Blessed are you, God of justice,
    for the many ways
    that you overlook my stubbornness
    and offer healing instead of punishment.
Teach me, God of unconditional love,
    how to forgive those who displease me,
    how to have mercy and compassion
    toward all who confront me.
Fill me with the gentleness of Jesus,
    who absorbed violence and anger
    and returned only love.
Amen.

Doing Time

For most of us, about the only way time gets our attention is by not being there in sufficient supply. But what a blessing it is never to have enough time! The alternative to not having enough time is having too much time on our hands.

Although we may complain and curse and feel overwhelmed because there aren't enough hours in the day, I suspect we would choose for our lives to be that way—if we had the choice—than in a condition where time was something we had to do. "Doing time" is the term we have created for being in prison.

But not only prisoners are condemned to do time. So are the sick whose ailments will be cured only by time, and so are those for whom even time provides no cure. The same is true when we are bored. Whatever our condition, however, we all want to grasp the fleeting moment of happiness or pleasure or relief or joy. These are the moments when we would like for time to stand still, and for there to be no time, only the present moment.

The eternalizing of the present moment is what we have been promised by God if we are faithful. God will give us a moment of unspeakable happiness and never take it away. Help us, Lord, to believe your promises and live in the time you give us so as to be ready for even greater gifts.

*B*lessed are you,
>God of our days and God of our nights,
>for you have clothed all of time
>>with the splendor of your glory.

Blessed are you,
>God of ordinary days and extraordinary graces,
>for you have created time itself,
>that we might better grasp your mystery
>>in its gradual unfolding.

Loving God,
>help me to see the wonders of your grace
>each and every time I share in the Eucharist.

Make every Eucharist extra-ordinary,
>every day filled with awe in your presence.

Amen.

In the Heart of God

The wise man said: "Say not: God is in my heart; but rather say: I am in the heart of God." Here we have two different worlds and two different ways of living faith and life. The one who says "God is in my heart" has the belief that the heart is somehow immense enough to contain God. Any time life brings disappointments such as death, desperation, failure—any time one's heart is broken—what happens to the house of God? Are its foundations shaken? If God is in my heart, then so are God's power and love and compassion and mercy. My sins tell me if God is in my heart; God is not in control of me.

But when I say: "I am in the heart of God," my world is enlarged to the size of God's world. There in God's heart, I am one with God and with all God's other children, including the poor, the sick, the unborn, and the stranger.

Help me, Lord God, to get outside my own heart, to break the shell that imprisons me and keeps you too small to be real, and too small to be worthy of my faith and love.

*L*ord, grant me a clean heart
  that I may act with honesty
  and serve you with courage.
Lord, fix my heart
  that with purity of act and intention
  I may be used by you.
For I am not worthy
  of all the blessings and graces
  you have bestowed upon me.
Give me a clean heart, Lord,
  and I will follow you.
Amen.

Movements in the Spiritual Life

Henri Nouwen, the late priest-writer from the Netherlands, wrote many books on the spiritual life. His book *Reaching Out* is one of his finest works. In this book he traces three movements in the spiritual life of individuals. They are: from loneliness to solitude, from hostility to hospitality, and from illusion to prayer.

He considers loneliness to be an essential part of the human condition, one we cannot escape even though we may have many friends. To be lonely in the midst of a crowd is an experience we have all had at one time or another. Besides, there are many things we have to do alone, such as deciding, dying, and sinning.

Loneliness can be very depressing, and produces a neediness that often leads to disillusionment. The neediness flows from the illusion that another human being can take away the loneliness. Perhaps another human being can distract us from our loneliness temporarily, but ultimately there are so many things we must face alone.

Solitude, on the other hand, is the condition of being comfortable with oneself alone. It is in solitude that the presence of God becomes felt. To know the presence of God is to begin to find the only real remedy for loneliness. Loneliness, hostility, and illusion are fairly common experiences. Nouwen helps us by treating them as launching pads for spiritual growth.

Spirit of God,
    in joy and sorrow,
    in activity and rest,
    in health and sickness,
    you uplift, renew, and re-create my life.
Your ways are not my ways,
    seldom can I anticipate what lies ahead.
Give me strength to trust in your direction
    away from loneliness and hostility.
Give me hope to hold on
    in the face of illusion.
Give me faith to know
    you are present and leading me to God.
Amen.

Liturgy as a Story

I found a remarkable statement in the course of some spiritual reading one day. It was from the book *Storytelling: Imagination and Faith* by William A. Bausch. Father Bausch states without reservation that "any true spirituality must be liturgical." He maintains that we have to take our own stories seriously, because they are our life. And we need to take the story of God seriously, because God's story is connected to our life too.

God's story and our story need to be learned, owned, contemplated, prayed, shared, and celebrated. It is in the liturgy that we not only hear and think about God's story of redemption as we find it in the Bible, but we are brought together as a community of faith, hope, and love. The liturgical year moves us, like paragraphs, from episode to episode in the story of Jesus. Our verses, songs, vestments, and decorations are all trappings for our ongoing celebration of God's story and ours.

We know we have been touched by grace, so we are bound to celebrate our story. I am sure the author had no intention of putting down personal spirituality, because it is formed by learning, thinking about, praying about, accepting as real, God's story and ours. But then what do you do with it? Unless it is shared and celebrated, a necessary human dimension is missing.

To share story in celebration is liturgy. Thank you, Father Bausch, for helping me understand why I am so personally committed to liturgical piety, and try to help others move in that direction. It's where real life is.

Jesus, my Master,
I did not accompany you
    as you healed the blind and the lame,
but you still call me to bind up wounds
    and to comfort the brokenhearted.
I did not sit with you
    as you taught your disciples,
but you still expect me to feed those
    who hunger for your truth.
You did not choose me to be an apostle,
    but you have sent me
    to serve my brothers and sisters.
You have inspired me not to write my story,
    but to proclaim your story within me.
Amen.

"In the Name of the Encouragement You Owe Me" (Philippians 2:1)

When Paul writes to the people at Philippi, he is straightforward and his words glisten with clarity. He points out how his work for Christ is his life, and how much joy they bring to him because of their faith. But he is aware of the divisions that exist among them, and how certain individuals are known by their conceit and rivalry. So he calls the people to greater unity and harmony.

He puts it in the form of an obligation they owe him. "In the name of the encouragement you owe me" he encourages them to be humble. From there he takes us into one of the most sublime passages in all of his writings. In it Jesus gives us the ultimate example of humility. "Though he was in the form of God, he did not deem equality with God something to be grasped at. . . . Rather, he emptied himself . . . obediently accepting even death, death on a cross." And God saw to it that his suffering was not in vain: "Because of this, God highly exalted him" (2:6–9).

The good news is that just as God rewarded Jesus for his humble obedience, so God will reward us. All the sacrifices we make to keep harmony in the community of faith will not be missed by God and we will be glad in the end we traded away our conceit. To encourage means to give someone the heart for it. Paul was demanding what he needed from them to have the heart for the important work he was doing. Don't we all need that from one another? It's so Christian.

*J*esus, our Shepherd,
  lead us out of our wanderings and weakness.
Set us on the path of holiness and wholeness.
Guard us against the lure of easy answers
  and quick fixes.
Strengthen us instead with patient endurance
  in our struggle to know you
  and conform to your image.
Attune us that we might recognize your voice
  and follow your Way.
Clear our hearts and minds.
Open the way for the gifts and fruits of your Spirit
  to become a reality in our life.
Amen.

How Do I Know I Love God?

How do I know I love God? Maybe there is no more important question. Father Hilary Ottensmeyer, O.S.B., answered simply by reviewing some ways we relate as persons, highlighting certain qualities of intimacy. Let me put them in the form of questions. It becomes a kind of self-examination that will lead us to the answer:

> Do I enjoy spending time with God, just passing time?
>
> Have I ever said or felt like saying to God: "God, I need to tell you who I am?"
>
> Do I not only speak to God, but listen to see if God has something to share?
>
> Do I feel a kind of mutual support, where I believe God thinks it's okay for me to be me, and for God to be God?

What goes on between persons is not all there is. Something has to also happen within a person:

> Do I experience feelings of closeness to God and safety being with God?
>
> Do I like God without having to work at it?
>
> Does my relationship with God bring me a kind of satisfaction?
>
> And do I consider this relationship important, of great value?

Answer "yes" to all these questions and we know we love God. If we are unsure on some of them or can't say yes, we know where we have to work to improve our love of God. Notice that one could use these same questions to review a relationship of love with another human being! And if we have such a relationship, we might have some feelings of gratitude to God for the gift of such a friend.

Body of Christ, nourish and feed
    my hunger for wholeness.
Blood of Christ, wash me clean
    from my sins and failings.
Open my mind to understand
    the fullness of the gift of your Eucharist.
Evoke in me a gratitude for your presence
    and a forgiving spirit toward all.
Unite me to all of humankind
    who share in the same forgiveness
    you offer a hungry thirsty world.
Make of me a sign of your presence
    to all I encounter this week.
Amen.

Sharing in the Prophetic Role of Jesus

In Baptism, the priest anoints new Christians and says: "As Christ was anointed Priest, Prophet, and King, so may you live always as a member of his body." The most intriguing role is that of prophet. How do we exercise our responsibility to be prophetic? In the early part of his public ministry, Jesus discovered a reality he put in these words: "No prophet is without honor except in his native place, among his own kindred, and in his own house" (Mark 6:5).

Put this together with the job description of the prophet in Jeremiah, and we can understand why people are reluctant to take on the role. Mostly what you get in return is anger, alienation, or just plain ignored. God told Jeremiah: "Look, today I am setting you over nations and over kingdoms, to tear up and to knock down, to destroy and overthrow, to build up and plant" (Jeremiah 1:10). Four of the six jobs are negative and destructive. No wonder when someone "speaks for God" (what prophet means) people get upset.

Jesus implies that we need to bring prophecy home. What would that look like? Maybe something like this: "Thus says the Lord God: 'No! You can't shack up with your girlfriend (boyfriend)!' " Or: "Thus says the Lord God: 'Go rent a good movie. Forget that X-rated one you were planning to see.' " Or: "Thus says the Lord God: 'Go get a job! You are out of college now and need to be on your own.' " And, for sure: "Thus says the Lord God: 'You are my beloved daughter (son), and I have loved you with an everlasting love.' "

God of endless love,
your truth is eternal, it never changes.
  Transform us in truth
    that our lives might speak to others
      of your love.
Inspire us to confront injustice in the world,
to promote your peace and reconciliation.
  Help us to faithfully heed your prophets
  who witness in spirit and truth.
Make us fearless prophets who will speak
when and where you send us.
  For your eternal truth sets us free,
    through Jesus our brother
    and the Holy Spirit.
Amen.

A Reflection on the Parable of the Weeds

In Matthew's Gospel, we often find difficult teachings. It is there, for instance, we find the parable of the weeds that were sown among the wheat. "The harvest is the end of the age, and the harvest workers are angels. Just as the weeds are gathered up and burned in the fire so the same thing will happen at the end of the age: the Son of Man will send out his angels to gather up out of his Kingdom all those who cause people to sin and all others who do evil things and they will throw them into the fiery furnace, where they will cry and gnash their teeth" (Matthew 13:39–42).

Since we are all sinners, it's a little frightening to read these threats. How can we possibly console ourselves and hope to escape this monstrous fate? Recognizing the reality and the power of sin, what do we do?

All through the Bible we are confronted with the reality of God's caring. One insight that helps me tremendously comes from the parable about the pearl of great price, which, once discovered, caused the merchant to sell all he had to buy it. If we ask the question: What is God's pearl of great price? I think the answer is: We are! And the price God paid was his own Son. Remember, we have already been judged. God has judged us to be of immense value, valuable enough to expose his only Son to death. Please feel valuable. The more valuable we feel, the less we will sin.

*W*eeds and wheat,
    O, God of kingdom harvesting,
    we are both.
Yet in your infinite mercy
    you embrace us, your saved sinners,
    opening us out to the grace-filled
        Spirit implanted deep within our souls.
Empowered by your Spirit,
    help us to grow into kingdom living
    where saint and sinner alike
        are welcomed and enfolded
           in your divine love.
Amen.

The Seven Secrets of Successful Catholics

In the September 1997 issue of *U.S. Catholic,* Paul Wilkes had an interesting article entitled "The Seven Secrets of Successful Catholics." These Catholics are successful because Catholicism is a framework for their lives and their actions. See if these seven secrets apply:

Successful Catholics stay close to the Eucharist. Without the Eucharist in their lives, these Catholics feel impoverished, isolated, empty. They are members of a faith community; they know they need the company of others on their life journey toward God. They rely on their conscience and good judgment—but never alone; life is a pilgrimage, not a prepackaged trip. They regularly do things that call them out of themselves—ministry, or some volunteer effort. They live in the moment, recognizing daily opportunities for holiness, and they use their sacramental imagination to discover God in everyday events.

Successful Catholics always remember that God is merciful and forgiving; they are no strangers to self-reflection: they recognize all too well their shortcomings, but they are confident that no matter how miserably they have behaved, they can never, ever exile themselves beyond the reach of God's love. They believe in prayer and pray regularly. Whatever their spirituality, successful Catholics consider prayer crucial to their moral well-being.

*D*ear Lord,
   life is not easy.
There are so many decisions to make
   and problems to solve.
Am I fair and honest at work?
Do I, as a parent, balance
   love and discipline?
Do I both affirm and challenge my friends?
I know that your love has saved me.
But that is only the beginning;
   I need to know how to live.
Give me then your wisdom
   that I may find the secrets
   to a successful life of Christian love.
Amen.

And There Went Paradise

Adam knew he was wrong. He tried to hide from God. When he was discovered and God called him to account, he wimped out and blamed Eve, and God. "It was the woman you put with me." Eve followed Adam's example and blamed the serpent. "The serpent tempted me and I ate" (Genesis 3:12–13). The serpent had no one to blame. But it was too late anyway. Once blaming entered the picture, there went paradise. As scholars try to determine the exact nature of the first human sin, maybe they ought to consider feigning innocence. I wonder what would have happened if they just owned up to it and asked forgiveness.

I doubt if we would still have paradise, however. What Adam and Eve did seems to be part of the human condition even before the Fall. Just be alert and watch people try to get off the hook by blaming others. Children do it. How many sisters have been blamed for their brothers' omissions? And vice versa? "She didn't do the dishes, so I didn't take out the trash." And there went paradise. . . . People often do it in cars. Have you ever heard a driver blame another with the horn? The lights? A scowl? A finger? People seem to need a scapegoat and, having found a likely victim, think the problem is solved. And there went paradise. . . .

Every time we finger someone else to get ourselves off the hook, we blow paradise away again. The alternative is to start taking responsibility for our actions.

Jesus,
    my life is so often drab and mundane.
I do my job, bear my responsibilities,
    carry my burdens.
It's not my fault I get so easily caught up in the
    routines and banalities of life
    and blame others for my shortcomings.
Arrest me for only a moment
    with the real consequences of my choices.
Help me to realize that,
    with the touch of your grace,
    I can be responsible for my life.
Amen.

When It's Safe to Be Free

Back in the sixties—some of us can remember—when young people and others were revolting against what they perceived as oppressive institutions, an insight developed which is expressed well in these words: "Freedom breeds responsibility; nonfreedom breeds rebellion."

As an institution tries to control the minds and actions of the people who identify with it, it loses exactly what it wants the most: control. In freedom a dream can grow into reality, as the people who share the dream take responsibility to make it happen.

Precisely the same thing happens between individuals. The more one tries to control the other, the more the one who is being forced under control rebels. When these individuals call each other friends, an element of tragedy seeps into the scene.

So when is it safe to be free? In the presence of a true friend. There is no other place where freedom and safety can coexist. To have such a friend, who makes it safe to be free, is one of life's greatest treasures. To be called a friend is to be called to responsibility, bred by a feeling of safety in a climate of freedom. And all of us have such a friend in Jesus, who said to his disciples: "I call you friends" (John 15:15).

You have visited this household, O God,
    in the living Word, made flesh,
        who is Christ our Savior.
Keep our ears attuned
    to the sound of Jesus' voice;
        steady our feet to follow in his path.
Through the gift of his loving friendship,
    strengthen us to choose the course
        of communion with you,
        discipleship in Christ,
        and covenant love with all peoples.
Amen.

Cut It Out, You Guys

I was at a restaurant the other day when three elderly ladies came in and sat at a table. One of the ladies needed extra help. All three were very well dressed and had just been to the hairdresser. Eventually a waitress appeared, came to the table where these dignified ladies waited, and said, "Have you guys decided what you want today?" No doubt the waitress was trying to be casually hospitable, but my reaction was not positive. I felt embarrassed, sad, and somewhat contemptuous of the clumsiness of this girl.

I harbored this contempt for a couple days, until confronted by a passage from the Sermon on the Mount. It was from the challenging section where Jesus contends that our holiness must exceed that of the scribes and Pharisees. Jesus implies that the leaders of the people are satisfied if no one kills another. They tend to be legalistic and Jesus wants more from his followers. He goes way beyond legalism. He condemns those who are angry with their brothers or sisters, those who call others bad names, and those who hold others in contempt.

He was about to announce the only law he would give us, namely, to love one another as he has loved us. How could anyone embrace his new law as a way of life if he was enjoying feelings of contempt for others or if he carried around in his heart a ball of anger that blocked all instinct to love?

Jesus, your saving suffering on the cross
    flows out over the ages,
        over all nations,
        over all of creation.
You lead us to greatness
    by planting a generous heart
        within the human spirit.
Give us the wisdom and
    guidance we need to look at life
        from the underside,
    that we might spend our days
        serving the least in imitation of you.
Amen.

Prayer Life Is Not Static

What is prayer, really? A direction I've taken is to look for "feeling" words in the Scriptures. Believe me, once you put your attention on such words, they jump out at you. Jesus, for instance, was angry when he tossed the moneychangers out of the Temple. Jesus wept over his friend Lazarus who had died. Jesus wept over the city of Jerusalem. Mary was frightened when the angel Gabriel came to announce she would be the Mother of God. "Do not be afraid" the angel said to her.

When I focus on these feeling words, the saints to whom I pray become more and more real, and I feel more and more connected to them. Sometimes the connection is so strong I cry. It always happens to me when I think of Mary at the cross. She must have longed for a word from Jesus. He was speaking. "I thirst." "Father, forgive them for they know not what they do." And to one of the thieves: "This day you shall be with me in paradise." Did he not have a word for his mother? Finally, he said: "Mother, here is your son." But he was not talking about himself, he was referring to John. Once more she found herself directed away from him. Another sword piercing her heart.

Maybe we ought to call this form of prayer the prayer of empathy. It works for me, even though it puts my attention on the saint and not directly on God. God comes in as an object of gratitude because God was present in all this, sustaining and gracing.

*F*ather, God, the Most High Judge,
Jesus, our Advocate, and
Holy Spirit, blessed Counselor,
    in you is the hope of the world.
Holy Mother Mary,
    and all the communion of saints,
    pray for us.
We thirst, we are afraid,
    we beg God's forgiveness.
Direct us to the source of life
    that we might be sustained
    in divine grace.
Amen.

The Smaller the World

I used to feel sorry for people who were not members of my family, did not have the opportunity to grow up on a farm, did not live in Hartford City, and didn't get to own a Daisy BB gun. Was my world small! As one grows up, one's world tends to get larger. I suppose one might even make a correlation between the size of one's world and the level of one's maturity.

As we read the Gospels, we discover that Jesus had trouble with people whose world was too small. And not only the establishment figures whose world was constricted by the Law, but even the apostles who remained attached to their notion of Messiah and their prejudices against Gentiles and women. Someone who objects to healing because it is a violation of the Sabbath lives in a very small world. So does someone who chases away a needy woman because she is a Canaanite. Or who objects to somebody casting out devils who is not one of the apostles.

People with very small worlds dot the landscape. We all know them. Mental health professionals tell us it is healthy to enlarge our world. Having broad interests is an alternative to burnout. But Jesus leads us into the largest world there is, the world of love. He led by word and by example. Remember when he stretched out his arms on the cross, he embraced with his love the whole world. When we have excluded no one from our love, our world is large enough.

God of growth and change,
  my life has become set
  in habits and patterns that control me.
I see myself in the harsh mirror
  polished by the mistakes and failures
    of my past,
  and framed by the fear that I cannot grow.
Send your Holy Spirit to warm my heart,
  to stretch my imagination,
  to quiet my fear.
With your Spirit to guide me,
  I can break old chains,
  think new thoughts,
  and become the person you call me to be.
Amen.

The Blessing of Routine

Over the July Fourth holiday, my routine of work and prayer gets totally upset. All that freedom seems so unfamiliar. I don't pray or produce very well. In our noncontemplative society, it's possible to experience feelings of guilt when our production is down. But when it comes to prayer and ministry, who's keeping score? Is there really some heavenly statistician keeping a record, so that someday we might be presented with our lifetime spiritual bouquet?

Our God is really more interested in relationships than statistics. Besides, love and intimacy are hard to measure.

Nevertheless, another insight this holiday weekend produces is the need for routine. Without a prayer routine, our prayer is dependent on personal initiative, and there are so many distractions. So thank God for the blessing of routine. Ancient religions understood all this, and that's why the official prayer of the Church is built around certain hours, like morning and evening prayer. So is Jewish prayer. Absence of a prayer routine could signal an absence of prayer.

Saint Thomas Aquinas defined *virtue* as the "habit of doing good." Routine produces habits of prayer. Thank God for the blessing of routine.

*C*reator, you are mindful of my every need,
    and fill my life with your abundant gifts.
Still my heart that I might see
    the needs of my brothers and sisters.
When I experience unforeseen pain,
    calm my spirit that I might trust
        your compassionate care.
When I am overwhelmed by the distraction
    of unexpected events in my life
        draw me to yourself as if it were
        my ordinary routine.
Amen.

Adam Wanted a Partner, Not a Pet

Most brides and grooms choose the story of the creation of woman to be read at their big event. I always wonder why. Obviously, they are sending some sort of message about themselves or their values by their choice. Of course you remember the story. Adam was given the task of naming all the animals and other creatures after God decided it was not good for the man to be alone. Adam could find no suitable partner among the other creatures. Adam didn't want a pet, he wanted a partner.

So God took one of his ribs and built it up into a woman. Adam was ecstatic when he saw her. "At last!" he exclaimed in his delight. "This one will be called woman, for out of 'her man' she was taken" (Genesis 2:23). Do you suppose that couples want this passage read because the most romantic thing a man could say to a woman at the time the story was written was, "You are my rib!"?

Maybe they understand Adam's comment about the woman being taken out of "her man" as the equalizer for the fact that the man named the woman. To name something is to possess it, to have dominion over it. The man named the woman "Eve." God named the man "Adam." But the man was referring to himself when he said out of "her man" she was taken. Even though Adam can say to Eve, "You're mine," he also says to her, "I'm yours." Adam wanted a partner, not a pet.

*L*oving God,
　　it was not enough for you to give me life,
　　to call me from nothingness to joy.
It was not enough for you
　　to bless me with gifts and talents,
　　to provide me with dreams
　　　　which my years could attain.
It was not enough
　　to surround me with family and friends
　　　　who call forth the best from me.
Beyond all these gifts, you give me yourself.
Allow me to live in union with you,
　　never divorcing myself from your presence.
Amen.

Community Building Works

I once spent two days sitting at the feet of M. Scott Peck, psychiatrist and author of several books, at a community building workshop. In his book *The Different Drum,* Scotty (that's what he insisted we call him) declared that every community—if it ever gets to community—goes through three inevitable stages. They are pseudocommunity, where everyone is nice; chaos, which is what it sounds like; and emptiness, which I will try to describe. Only after people have experienced these stages can community happen. Pseudocommunity is that stage where everybody is pleasant. It doesn't last long. Chaos is filled with subtle and not-so-subtle attacks, sarcasm, anger, preaching, attempts at converting, self-pity, criticism, bellyaching, name-calling, analyzing, and many other forms of self-centered words, body postures, and behaviors.

The emptiness stage is when all this stops and the ingredients of chaos are no longer present in the group. Our group began the process of emptying when one of the group shared a dream he had the first night of the seminar. It was so powerful we were all stunned. Then people suddenly felt free to share some of their personal stories. They were stories of pain, but they turned out to be precious gifts. A kind of holy silence enveloped the group. Suddenly we were persons to one another. Broken, battered, vulnerable persons, just as we all are. We came to community. Don't ask me to define it. When you get there, you know it. Scott Peck believes this process has real promise for world peace. I suspect it has to happen in families and parishes and other natural groupings first. But first comes the emptiness.

*L*ord God, my Savior,
   my horizons are too narrow.
Expand my vision.
Allow me to remember that you have a plan
   to reform the world
   into your perfect kingdom.
Lead me to trust that Jesus will return,
   and his power will sweep away evil
   and lift all our hearts to your praise.
Instill in me the patience to meet people
   on their own terms and to empty myself
   of all that impedes sharing your presence.
Amen.

A Time for a "Change of Heart"

Pope John Paul II wrote his dissertation on Max Scheler, a profound thinker who came from Christian-Jewish parentage, and was really a kind of misfit all his life. He wrote a book, *On the Eternal in Man,* in which he deals at length with the subject of repentance. What good is repentance, he asks, since it cannot change the past? And he answers: "Repentance is a form of self-healing of the soul," which is "in fact its only way of regaining its lost powers."

"Repenting is equivalent to re-appraising part of one's past life and shaping for it a mint-new worth and significance. People tell us that repentance is a senseless attempt to drive out something 'unalterable.' But nothing in this life is 'unalterable' in the sense of this argument. Even this 'senseless' attempt alters the 'unalterable' and places regretted conduct or attitude in a new relation within the totality of one's life, setting it to work in a new direction.

"It is not the repented but only unrepented guilt that holds the power to bind and determine the future. Repentance kills the life-nerve of guilt's action and continuance. It drives motive and deed—the deed with its root—out of the living centre of the Self, and thereby enables life to begin, with a spontaneous, virginal beginning, a new course springing forth from the centre of the personality which, by virtue of the act of repentance, is no longer in bonds" (*On the Eternal in Man,* Shoestring, 1972, pp. 41–42).

Jesus, Healer and Reconciler,
    touch my life and make me whole;
    restore me to full union with you
    and my brothers and sisters.
Where there is suffering,
    enfold all in your healing embrace.
Where there is evil,
    reconcile all in the power of love.
Where there are boundaries,
    liberate all to risk crossing them
    to include rather than exclude.
Where there is doubt,
    shower all with the hope
    of your transforming, healing grace.
Amen.

Winners and Losers—So Often

In the story of the parting of the Red Sea and escape of the Israelites from the approaching army of the Egyptians, the Egyptian army, remember, was drowned when the walls of water fell on them—winners and losers. While the Israelites celebrated their liberation from captivity and the promise of entering a new land of peace and prosperity, Egyptian families were mourning the loss of sons and fathers and the promises that died with them.

According to an old rabbinic story, when the chosen people escaped from Egypt and made it through the harrowing crisis of the Red Sea (imagine the suspense if you were watching from above and did not know the outcome), the angels began to celebrate. In their joy they went to the God of Israel to join in their celebration. But they found God weeping, and scolding them. "How can I celebrate when my children are drowning?" So the rabbis tell the story.

The Scriptures tell us: "Rejoice with those who rejoice! Weep with those who weep!" Even God can't seem to do both at the same time. Lord, help us to be mindful of the losers as we join the winners in their celebration.

*L*ord Jesus,
>how often have I questioned
>whether or not you are in the midst
>of my life's trials and tribulations?

Like the Israelites of old,
>I grumble when things are difficult,
>forgetful of how often you have rescued me.

Help me, loving Jesus,
>in life's continuous conflicts
>to remember always that, win or lose,
>you are with me in my rejoicing
>and in my weeping.

Amen.

Follow Me! Again and Again

When Jesus first said "Follow me!" to Peter, Peter protested that he was a sinful man and that Jesus should leave him. Not intimidated by sinfulness, Jesus told him he would be catching people from now on, not fish. Peter rose to a leadership position with the apostles, but it was probably compromised by his elaborate display of sinfulness, when, after he had boasted about his fidelity to Jesus, he denied him three times. This was not a denial before a judge who could hurt Peter, but before a girl warming herself by a bonfire.

Jesus gave Peter a chance to feel forgiven for his denials and at the same time entrusted him with much responsibility. Jesus loved and needed that sinner. Three times Jesus gave Peter a chance to express his love for Jesus and each time asked him to feed Jesus' sheep and lambs. All this was followed by those familiar words, "Follow me!"

Jesus never stopped inviting. Even the apostles needed several invitations, it seems. Most of us can identify with them. Sometimes we feel less than enthusiastic about being a disciple. We are distracted by our own words, our relationships, or our sins. This Gospel story tells us there really is no excuse, not even sinfulness. God needs us loved sinners to make God's Word available and God's love real in our world. The invitation "Follow me" is ringing in our ears and tugging at our hearts.

*L*ord Jesus,
  you entrusted to Peter
  the care of your Church.
Watch over our Holy Father,
  as he seeks to walk in Peter's footsteps.
Guide him with your Spirit of wisdom.
Guard him with a faith that is solid as a "rock."
Lord Jesus,
  help me to see in your chief shepherd
  a sign of your own abiding love and protection.
Help me to be receptive to your teachings
  and open to the inspiration of your example
  that he embodies.
Amen.

He Walks with Me

One of the participants of my RENEW session related his impression of a priest he heard who asserted that many Catholics do not have a personal relationship with Jesus. He never defined what he meant by "personal relationship," but I suspect it means that Jesus was close by, walking as a companion on the spiritual journey. And I presume it means one is able to carry on something of a conversation as well. It would seem that one's imagination would also be engaged and one would have a fairly clear picture of what this Jesus looks like. It would be interesting to have someone with a personal relationship with Jesus describe what he looks like. Would he have a beard? Would he dress in the clothes of his time or ours? Is he handsome? Smiling?

If we as Catholics lack this personal relationship, what is it that we have? We certainly have faith in Jesus, and we sense his presence in very many ways, thanks to the faith. Let us list some of the ways. Jesus is present each time a sacrament is celebrated. There is Jesus justifying in Baptism, nourishing in Holy Communion, healing in the Anointing of the Sick, forgiving in the confessional, imparting the Holy Spirit in Confirmation, commissioning in Holy Orders, and sanctifying in Matrimony. Besides, we find Jesus in the reading of the Holy Scripture, in eucharistic worship, in each other, and in the needy.

If we were to describe the Jesus we Catholics encounter as a result of our faith in him, it would be a radically different picture from the sentimental one above.

*J*esus, my Lord,
I believe you are truly present
    in the bread and wine of the Eucharist.
I believe you are with me as the same Lord
    who formed the world,
    who healed the sick,
    who lifted up the poor.
As I adore you with the eyes of faith,
    allow my concern to extend
    beyond the appearances of bread and wine.
Lead me to serve the poor,
    care for the sick,
    and cherish the world you have made.
Amen.

The Hazards of Coddling Anger

Anger is one of those emotions we all know. Jesus knew it, and sometimes even displayed it. I suspect he was angry when he cursed the fig tree and made it wither. There's no doubt he was angry when he drove the moneychangers out of the Temple. If it wasn't anger behind some of his words to the Pharisees, it must have been a stronger emotion. Yet Jesus is the one who encouraged us to "Be angry, and sin not." So we're not necessarily talking about sin.

Reflecting on our own experience of anger, doesn't it sometimes lead us to places where we aren't very proud to be? Sometimes it leads to a desire to punish, and sometimes the punishment we dish out is more severe than the injury we've received, like Lamech in the Book of Genesis: "I killed a man for wounding me, a boy for striking me" (Genesis 4:23). Usually, it leads to a false sense of self-righteousness, where we are totally correct, and the one who angered us is totally wrong. Nobody's that innocent. Or it makes us focus on the faults of the one who made us angry—and boy, are they easy to find! Nobody's all bad, but anger deceives us, because it makes us come to such conclusions.

Psychologists tell us that anger is a reflected feeling. People who make us angry usually display some fault we have ourselves but won't admit. Wouldn't it be something if we could use our anger to know ourselves and improve ourselves, rather than as an excuse to clobber somebody else?

*Cast Out
the Evils
of Violence*

*L*ord Jesus Christ,
>we proclaim you the Prince of Peace.
>You have told us,
"I leave you peace, my peace I give you,"
>and you bid us to share with one another
>>the gift of your peace.
Remove from our world the scourge of war.
Free us from angers and jealousies,
>from festering resentments,
>and covetous greed.
Cast out the evils of violence and hatred
>that plague the human heart,
>and fill us with your own divine Spirit
>>of peace, love, and forgiveness.
Amen.

How About a Fresh Image of God?

In his book *A Grief Observed,* C. S. Lewis remembers his biggest temptation as he tried to recover from his wife Joy's death. He was in his fifties when he married and it lasted less than a year, because Joy developed cancer and died very quickly. He said it was not that he was tempted to believe there was no God, but to believe such awful things about God. He was tempted to blame God for the grief he had so much trouble carrying. No one is more blamed than God. In some ways this could be a tribute, professing faith in the tremendous power of God. But it could also be an insult, and this is what worried Lewis. He did not want to accuse God of not caring.

The Song of Solomon is a poetic picture of a young couple on their honeymoon. The tender words and images are immensely beautiful. In the story God is the bridegroom, and God's people are the bride. This God is not cruel or vindictive, jealous or angry. This God is the passionate lover, loyal and tender, and overwhelming in graciousness.

God is also a precious baby who grew up and went about doing good, and was compared to a shepherd who would never abandon a lost sheep. You know the rest of the story. The people God sent Jesus to save killed him. But God raised him up on the third day to show us how death is not the final reality of life. Wouldn't it be wonderful if we could keep an affectionate image of God inside us and thereby become more like God— and everybody could tell?

My God, where are you?
Troubles and pain press me down
    without any hope of relief.
I remember the days when my life was a joy,
    when I felt your presence
    and exalted in your light.
Now there is only emptiness
    and the doubt that you really care.
Turn then to me with strength,
    allow me to believe you are still with me.
If I cannot touch your peace
    let me know I am not forgotten.
If I can only grieve,
    then accept these tears as my prayer.
Amen.

Making Philosophy 101 Practical

One of the first things I learned in Philosophy 101 was this basic principle: Whatever is received is received according to the mode of the receiver. (*Quidquid recipitur, ad modum recipientis recipitur*—for you Latin scholars.) This was fairly meaningless to me at the time, but I have become more and more convinced of the important truth this basic principle holds for all of us. For example, how many times have you given someone a message and he or she received something you didn't send?

Sometimes what is received is received according to the mode of the receiver. When everything is going wrong and some of it is serious, it's hard to hear someone complaining about his or her tiny, insignificant problem. Didn't get his way, poor baby! How hard it is to be compassionate when one is in pain. How many nasty responses or uncharacteristic barbs come from a bad mood?

This subject leads us into a consoling conclusion about our God. God doesn't have moods and is never confused. God is not supersensitive in the sense that God is easy to offend. God is a great receiver of messages. We can be confident in prayer because our God fits the ancient proverb: A friend is one to whom one may pour out all the contents of one's heart, chaff and grain together, knowing that the gentlest of hands will take and sift it, keep what is worth keeping, and with the breath of kindness blow the rest away.

*B*lessed are you, Lord God,
>flood us with your grace.
Rescue us from the trap of false humility,
>the snare of judging others,
>the blindness of our ego.
Guard us from judging others
>by their words alone
>and guide us to treat others always
>>with kindness and fairness.
Enflame us and set us free to love
>without limit our sisters and brothers
>who come before us poor and naked,
>>hungry and thirsty,
>>imprisoned, sick, and sorrowful.
Amen.

The Squelch of the Apostles

I have a cousin who was hired by an oil company in Houston to figure out a way to get out the 40 to 50 percent of remaining oil in wells that have stopped being productive. I said to Steve, "What is it like to go to work in the morning knowing that you aren't going to solve the problem hundreds of engineers have failed to solve in the last sixty years?" He replied, "Father, have you stamped out sin?" It's one of my favorite squelches.

Jesus did that to the apostles. When Peter replied to the question "Who do you say that I am?" with "The Messiah of God," Jesus told the apostles that he must suffer, be rejected by the leaders of their religion, and be killed. On the third day he would rise. They expected the Messiah to be a conquering hero who would restore the sovereignty of Israel, kick out the Romans, and perhaps even give them a free meal now and then. It was beyond their imagination to include suffering and death.

Jesus also told them that he would not be alone in his suffering. Anyone who wants to be his disciple must suffer, too, by taking up the cross every day. The apostles were looking for glory, for seats at his right and his left when he entered into his glory. You mean that's not going to happen? Oh no! Now there's a squelch. Do we find the crosses other people lay on us an opportunity to respond in charity as the mark of a true disciple, or do we respond cross for cross?

Prayer of Charles de Foucauld

*F*ather, I abandon myself into your hands;
   do with me what you will.
Whatever you may do, I thank you;
   I am ready for all, I accept all,
   let only your will be done in me,
   and in all your creatures—
   I wish no more that this, O Lord.
Therefore will I trust you always
   though I may seem to be lost
   and in the shadow of death,
I will not fear, for you are ever with me,
   and will never leave me to face my perils alone.
Amen.

Keep Those Family Stories Alive

At Thanksgiving, when my family converged at the parish house from Kentucky, Georgia, and several places in Indiana, I wondered how I could keep them from getting bored over the holiday. Not to worry! They did not depend on me for entertainment. We sat around the table and told family stories. Most of the stories have been told over and over. The stories that had to do with parents who are gone were quite poignant, but most of the stories brought much laughter. One we all love to tell, for example, involves my mother and an aggressive buck sheep which years ago on the family farm sent her flying through the air. Dad got there and rescued her, but she had some bruises. It's one of those events that was not funny at the time, but later seemed hilarious.

Treasure your family stories. Tell them over and over. Add the new ones as they happen. They are never boring and grow more interesting the more often they are told. From what evidence we can produce, it seems that Mary, the mother of Jesus, told family stories. And Luke wrote them down in the first chapter of his Gospel. She told him about the angels, the shepherds, the wise men. She told him about Herod and becoming a refugee. She told him about her feelings as all this was happening. It's a family story that has been told and retold, put to music, and never grows old or boring. Probably because Jesus is our brother and his family stories are our stories too. Let's keep telling them.

Good and gracious God,
     as you graced the family
of Jesus, Mary, and Joseph,
     you have touched our families
       with holy love.
Where we fail to see it,
     open our eyes.
When we suffer from hurts,
     renew in us your Spirit.
Strengthen us to be examples of holiness,
     to remember our family stories,
    to tell them with love and fondness,
      in communion with the one story
      that defines the story of your Church.
Amen.

From Ancestor Worship to the Feast of All Saints

While preparing a homily for a funeral Mass, I was suddenly struck by the thought: How would we be acting in this moment of grief if we lived twenty-five hundred years ago? Even if we were devout Hebrews, the probability of having a strong faith in life after death would be very low. It took a long time for people of faith to come to believe in life after death. In the Second Book of Maccabees, written very late, there is a consciousness of not only life after death, but reward and punishment in that life. "If he were not expecting the fallen to rise again, it would have been useless and foolish to pray for them in death. But if he did this with a view to the splendid reward that awaits those who had gone to rest in godliness, it was a holy and pious thought" (2 Maccabees 12:44–45).

In the Gospels we find Jesus arguing with the Sadducees, who did not believe in the resurrection of the body. What made faith in life after death explode into conviction among Christians was what happened to Jesus himself. He died, was buried, and rose again! As Paul taught with such directness, those who identify with Jesus in his death and burial will also share his resurrection. Baptism is the effective sign of this identification. In our funeral rites, we make much of how a deceased person was coupled with Jesus through Baptism and therefore shares in the resurrection. All the promises of life everlasting made by Jesus are now fulfilled for this happy soul. And so, while we grieve at our loss, we celebrate with a sense of real joy.

God,
I cannot imagine the
   wonders of your desire to be one with me
   nor the sweet joy of your heavenly home.
I struggle to see your kingdom on earth
   in the presence of the sinners and saints,
   the poor and the rich,
   the beautiful and the wild ones
      of this human family.
Open me to discover you in the
   faces of my brothers and sisters:
      those who are loving and lovable,
      those who are unacceptable and sinful—
In order that I might be comfortable with all
   at the feast of love in your kingdom.
Amen.

"Set Your Heart on the Greater Gifts"

At many weddings we hear the reading from Paul about love being the greatest of the virtues. The reading begins: "But strive for the greater gifts. And I will show you a still more excellent way" (1 Corinthians 12:31). Even though I have read and heard this text a thousand times, it never entered my mind to ask, "More excellent way than what? Gifts greater than what?"

Paul was writing to the Corinthians about the variety of gifts with which God has enriched the Church. These included "the utterance of wisdom . . . the utterance of knowledge . . . healing . . . prophecy . . . the working of miracles" (12:7–11). He concludes this chapter by asking a series of questions which show that not all have every gift. Then he says to set your heart on the greater gifts. I snapped to attention. An insight, no less.

The greater gift is love. Greater than working miracles, healing the sick, and speaking prophecies is: being patient and kind! Not being jealous or boastful! Not being arrogant or rude! Not insisting on your own way! Not being irritable or resentful! Not keeping a record of wrongs! God gives gifts of healing, prophecy, administration, and interpretation to special people for the welfare of the whole community and these are precious gifts. The greater gift, however, is one we can all embrace and enjoy and practice—love.

Paul cautions: "Now I know in part; then I shall understand fully, even as I have been fully understood" (12:12). It's exciting to enlarge the knowing-in-part a little with a treasured insight now and then. Thank you, Lord.

*B*lessed are you, Word of life,
    for you speak to my heart.
Blessed are you, Word of truth,
    for you enlighten my mind.
Blessed are you, Word made flesh,
    for you come to me with words of love.
Stir in me a keen longing
    to encounter you in the Holy Scriptures.
Strengthen my faith in your Word.
Help me to be attentive to your voice
    each and every time your Word is proclaimed.
May I always listen
    with open heart and lively faith.
Amen.

"Be Angry, And Sin Not"

Anger usually tells much more about ourselves than it does about the person who made us angry. I remember reacting very violently to a colleague who called me a chicken. We shouted at each other and made wild accusations for a few minutes before we realized we were grown men acting like children and apologized to each other. Later, when I was talking with a counselor, I righteously told him about the experience, expecting friendly support. Instead, he accepted my anger and said calmly, "What if he would have called you a communist? Would that have made you angry?"

"No."

"Why not?"

"Because it isn't true."

Wham! I suddenly realized my anger revealed a hidden doubt about the quality of my courage. I could no longer enjoy my anger or feel mistreated because I knew I had to deal with some uncomfortable truth about me that my anger had exposed.

Lord, give us the willingness to discover what our anger tells us about ourselves, rather than punish the people who have aroused us to anger so that we can follow your imperative: "Be angry, and sin not!"

*L*ord Jesus,
>   there is much that makes me afraid
>   and causes me anger.
I fear sickness, the loss of money,
>   rejection by my peers,
>   bad decisions by my children,
>   violence to my person and to my family.
My fear forces me to move in small circles,
>   always on guard against attack,
>   suspicious of whatever is unfamiliar.
My anger may have some basis,
>   but it cannot be my master.
Give me your love
>   that I may uncover the basis for my anger
>   and remove the fears that constrict my life.
Amen.

In the World, But Not of the World

Jesus prayed for his disciples, "I ask you not to take them out of this world, but to protect them from the evil one." When John uses the word *world,* it often means those forces of violence, deceit, and self-centeredness which are opposed to the Gospel of Jesus. The prayer of Jesus was answered for his first disciples, for they have a splendid record of courageously confronting and often converting the world. Modern-day disciples need Jesus praying for them just as much as the early disciples.

Much is said about the forces of evil in our world. Many hands are raw from all the wringing. It's easy to begin a list of such evils, but hard to complete the list because the forces of destruction and the evidence of decadence are so numerous. Life has become so cheap. Consider the murder of the fourteen-year-old boy who owed $45 on a drug debt. His killer, when confronted by the police about killing over such a small debt, retorted, "It's been done for less." The legality of abortion tends to dull the sensibilities of people regarding the sacredness of the lives of others. We used to curse or spit when another aggravated us. Now we shoot.

Suddenly, the call of Jesus to love as he has loved gives us some hope. Love drives out fear. May we acknowledge our status as disciples of Jesus and remember, Jesus prays that we may be protected from the evil one.

*T*ake our fears, O Loving God,
    and gather them into your embrace.
Transform them into patient endurance,
    courage, and compassion.
Use them to open us
    to surrender our whole self to you.
Inspire in us a holy awe of your majesty
    that we might give glory
    to the works of your creation—
        the roaring seas, the soaring mountains,
        the raging fire, and the quaking of the earth.
Most of all, grant that we might give you
    praise for the whisper of wind,
        the song of the dove,
        the laughter of a child.
Amen.

It's Not a Sin to Ask Questions

Job is the book of the Bible somebody wrote when God asked: "Tell me the story of how a good man suffers." Job lost everything, including his family and his property and his health. Like any of us would be, he was devastated. And in his pain he cried out: "Perish the day on which I was born, the night when they said, 'The child is a boy.' Why did I not perish at birth, come forth from the womb and expire? Wherefore did the knees receive me, or why did I suck at the breasts?" (Job 3:2, 3)

These are the words of a holy man in agony. Nothing he felt and none of his questions compromised his holiness. Feelings are neither good nor bad, they just are. It's not a sin to ask questions. Sometimes, however, in our pain we ask questions to which there are no answers. And Job seems to be doing just that. Once these are out of our system, maybe we can ask some questions that do have answers, questions like: How is God expecting me to grow in my faith as a result of this suffering? How can I respond to these awful events in a way that will improve me as a person?

Bad moments will come in our life as they came in Job's. May we use his story to help us keep our holiness despite the nasty feelings that often accompany suffering.

*T*hough destruction shouts its voice,
    and darkness looms overhead,
  your creative Word
    casts a lasting power,
      O God of heaven and earth.
When sickness grips us,
    when suffering comes upon us,
  instill in us your living Word,
    that in Jesus Christ
      who bore the cross for us,
  we are led to the fullness of our baptism,
    a faith and glory
      that lasts with you
  forever and ever.
Amen.

Down in the Dumps, and Out Again

I don't usually get depressed. And that's partly because I don't usually worry about money. But one July our parish had to confront some things that were depressing. Our building fund pledges were not coming in as we expected. Our regular Sunday giving had not increased according to projections and was not keeping up with very low inflation. Cost overruns on the building threatened our credit—and to exceed our line of credit meant a very difficult face-to-face encounter with the bishop. What would he say? Would he say he had better get somebody in here who will inspire the people to give? Depressing.

And then I read a quote from the late Archbishop Oscar Romero of El Salvador: "It is wrong to be sad. Christians cannot be pessimists. Christians must always nourish in their hearts the fullness of joy. Try it, brothers and sisters; I have tried it many times and in the darkest moments, when slander and persecution were at their worst: to unite myself intimately with Christ, my friend, and to feel a comfort that all the joys of the earth do not give— the joy of feeling oneself close to God, even when humans do not understand oneself. It is the deepest joy the heart can have."

I felt the wrongness about being sad and reached for the joy. I was glad this man said these words so I could use them when I needed them. Oscar Romero was gunned down while celebrating Mass. He must have felt horribly threatened, and he could still speak these words. That's holiness. Some have it; others just yearn.

*J*esus, my Messiah and Lord,
I possess so much more than you did
   in your earthly ministry.
I do not beg for food
   or search for a place to sleep.
I travel in comfort and clothe myself
   more for style than necessity.
Allow me to see in your poverty
   a call to place my trust in God.
Allow me to recognize in your homelessness
   an invitation to be thankful
   for what I possess.
Allow me to find in your lack of worldly power
   a love for the weak
   and dispossessed among us.
Amen.

Who Do You Think You Are?

Who were you before you were male or female? Who were you before you were named? Who were you before you went from baby to toddler to child, to adolescent and adult? Before you could smile or cry, crawl or walk? Who were you the first day you attended school, got your first report card, graduated? Did you know who you were on your first date? When you were married? Divorced? Got your first job? Who do you think you are? We could probably make a long list of what we are not, but none of this really answers the question of who we are. So how do we discover who we are? Are there classes or manuals or exercises? What does it take?

It takes a big step from self-concern to concern for the common good. It takes a kind of Copernican revolution for us to realize the world does not revolve around us the way we thought it did as a child. A businessperson living up to the promise of quality products or service discovers something about who he or she is. Doctors and nurses participate in the alleviation of suffering through healing, and their sense of satisfaction reveals a portion of their identity. The day firefighters save a life they have almost reached the answer to the question of who they are.

But even all these sometimes heroic activities do not thoroughly answer the question. If you decide you are anything but a beautiful creature, beloved of God, God's unique treasure, redeemed by Christ, and full of goodness and promise, yet fallen, you still haven't found you. God help us all.

> *Lord God,*
> *You*
> *Define Me*

*L*ord God,
　　you define who I am.
You call me out of my lethargy each day,
　　　　promising a new way of being,
　　　　a place of peace and harmony.
You set upon my heart a vision of hope,
　　　where the blind will see, the deaf will hear,
　　　　　and the mute will sing;
　　　where there will be no more thirst
　　　　in this desert of my dry spirit.
You sent your only Son to prepare me,
　　　to hear the cries of those in need,
　　　to see the beauty of all your creation,
　　　to speak your word of love to all I meet.
Pour your grace of compassion upon me
　　　until I overflow with love
　　　　　for my brothers and sisters everywhere.
Amen.

Got a Better Definition of Love?

One of my dear friends, a professor of family life, gave me a description of love many years ago which I have not been able to improve. He said love is being alert to the needs of others and being willing to make sacrifices to meet the needs perceived.

One of our contemporary Protestant theologians describes Jesus as "a man for others." Jesus went before us and gave us a model of a loving human life. He was continually alert to the needs of others and made the supreme sacrifice to meet the desperate need for salvation of all people, whom he viewed as his friends. At the same time, Jesus was able to go into the desert and pray, to meet his own spiritual needs, and fortify himself for his other-directed life. He was able to relax with friends like Martha and Mary and Lazarus. He also confronted with great force and courage those religious leaders of his time who were misleading the people.

Maybe Jesus took care of his personal needs for silence with the Father and fun with his friends because he loved himself and knew he had needs he had to meet too. Jesus showed us a balanced human life. One of the ways to discover how balanced our human life is (and also to discover how Christian it is) is to ask ourselves how often we are alert to our own needs compared to how often we are alert to the needs of others.

*H*oly God of covenant,
    I bless you for the grace
    you are as Savior and Lord,
        Son of God, Jesus Christ.
Holy God of mystery,
    I bless you for the love
    you are as Father and Creator,
        source of life and every good gift.
Holy God of love,
    I bless you for the fellowship
    you form as Holy Spirit,
        bond of unity and communion.
May my faith in you, God of understanding,
    inspire me always to balance my life
    with an awareness to the needs of others.
Amen.

"The Lord Is Kind and Merciful"

Kyrie eleison. These are Greek words that mean "Lord, have mercy." They were part of the very early liturgies in the Christian church, when the common language was Greek and Caesar ruled the world. Through the violence of his peerless army, he established what was known as the "Pax Romana." This was peace under the equivalent of martial law. This was not the peace brought about by kindness and mercy, as expressed by the Psalmist.

The early Christians rejected the power of Caesar, who had been divinized and was addressed as "Lord." So in their worship they began to exclaim, *Kyrie, eleison! Christe, eleison!* But the Lord was not Caesar; the Lord was Christ! No wonder the Romans persecuted the Christians! They refused to pay homage because their consciences told them it was idolatry.

They knew their need for mercy because of their sinfulness. But they knew Caesar was not their savior and had no power to provide their ultimate needs. Yet today Christians proclaim Jesus as Lord. May we all remember that Jesus' agenda was the proclamation of the kingdom of God and, to be faithful, all his disciples make the establishment of the kingdom their agenda. Kindness and mercy are critical elements.

This tells us what fantastic power we have. More power than armies, more power than the most sophisticated weapon. We have the power to make God present! May we adjust our lives, our words, our facial expressions and tone of voice, so that our friends and relatives can say: "The Lord is kind and merciful, and I believe that more now, because so are you!"

*B*lessed are you,
> compassionate God,
>> for the love which we do not deserve,
>> yet which is poured out on us so lavishly.

Blessed are you,
> God of mercy,
>> for the way that you always protect
>> the poor and those most vulnerable.

Blessed are you,
> God, who suffers with us
>> in Jesus your Son.

Fill our hearts with your love;
> stir up within us that same compassion,
>> that same pity for the helpless,
>> which you have revealed
>> fills your own divine heart.

Amen.

On Telling the Truth

"Honesty is the best policy." So goes the slogan. And it's a good one. Notice, however, that it tells us about policy, not virtue. According to Webster's Dictionary, *policy* means "a course of action, guiding principle, or procedure considered to be expedient, prudent, or advantageous." When we put honesty on the list of virtues, however, it is down the list. Remember, Saint Paul said that faith, hope, and love are the most important, and the greatest of these is love.

It doesn't take much imagination to figure out how honesty can be a violation of love. To tell the truth about someone to his or her face with honesty as the only measure of our words is to flirt with the creation of an enemy. Few can stand the kind of damage brutal honesty can cause the ego. To tell the truth about somebody to somebody else can be a sin. It is called detraction. We all know it is a sin to tell a lie about somebody. That's called calumny. People who enjoy gossip often don't realize it is usually detraction, an action requiring repentance and forgiveness.

Funny thing about those who appeal to the policy of honesty as a virtue: Most of the honest things they reveal are negative—and therefore destructive. If only we had a passion for using honesty to reveal the good things about people. People would feel so good . . . the goodness God saw when God looked on creation.

*F*rom the depths we cry out
    to you, O God of goodness and love.
Hear us, as we lay before you
      the pain and suffering of this world.
         (Name the suffering of the world
         for which you pray.)
Take these struggles and transform them
      that they might be a source of wisdom
      and truth for your people.
As our hearts are filled with good intentions,
      change us and turn us around
      that we might become a sign of
         your goodness,
            your mercy,
               your peace.
   Amen.

Discovering Who You Are

"For all you do, this Bud's for you." "You deserve a break today." "Be all that you can be!" People who create commercials know what we value. And this is nothing new. From the time of Socrates, whose motto was "Know thyself," to Polonius, who advised his son, "This above all: to thine own self be true," to Frank Sinatra, who sang about how he wanted to do it "my way," we have centered our attention on self.

Listen to the formula Jesus gives us to find out who we are: "He who seeks only himself brings himself to ruin, whereas he who brings himself to naught for me discovers who he is" (Matthew 10:38). To bring oneself to "naught" means to bring oneself to zero. Then, in that emptiness, there is a possibility of filling the space with the mind and heart of Jesus. We even pray for this in the preface of the Mass for Ordinary Time: "That you might see and love in us what you see and love in Christ."

Maybe some of Paul's words take on a new and fuller meaning as we reflect on what it means to bring oneself to naught. He encouraged the Philippians to "have that mind in you which was in Christ Jesus" (Philippians 2:5). And finally, totally emptied, he exclaimed, "I live, not I, but Christ lives in me" (Galatians 2:20).

Perhaps we were already aware that one of the ways we have the Risen Christ regularly in our midst is through his presence in one another. The search for self ends when we find Christ and let him take over.

*C*hrist, our light,
    radiate your light into our lives
    that we might become a light for others.
Rising Son of God,
    reconcile us to your created world
    that we might honor the earth
        and all creatures.
Flame of God's unwavering promises,
    redeem us, forgive us, save us,
    that we might bring this good news to others.
Christ of history, fulfillment of time,
    enlighten our hearts and our souls
    that we might pulse with God's love.
Christ of the cosmos,
    ignite our imagination
    that your kingdom might shine through us.
Amen.

Small Group Sharing—There Is No Substitute

People who have been through any of the renewal programs of the last few decades have discovered the only way to keep the experience alive is to follow though with like-minded people in small groups which meet regularly. This is true of Marriage Encounter, Cursillo, Christ Renews His Parish, as well as the RENEW process.

I made a Cursillo and for years have continued to "group." We report on how our prayer and study went over the past week. We talk about our successes and failures, although we usually don't call them either. One of the features of each session is to share the "close moments" of the week. Some of these are joyful and some are sad. Finally, we state our plan for the near future and some special intentions we want to include in our closing prayers. One of the men said after a few weeks of this routine: "I thought I was fairly faithful in my prayers until I had to account for them to someone else."

In small groups people become church to one another. There is an intimacy and fellowship developed which could never happen in a larger group assembly, such as a Sunday Mass. When small groups exist in a parish, however, Sunday Masses suddenly become more intense celebrations and there is more participation. Give some serious thought to joining a small group now. You have nothing to lose but that unhealthy sense of isolation.

Jesus, Head of the Church,
    at times I feel the tension
    between my own ideas
    and the beliefs of others
       in the Catholic community.
I realize that we do not all see you
    in exactly the same way.
Help me to be flexible.
Without denying my own vision,
    allow me to live in the shared tradition
       of my Church.
You have made me an individual
    but you have called me
    to be part of a community.
Give me the grace to join my voice
    to the song of your people.
Amen.

God Does Not Have a Consumer Mentality

A person with a consumer mentality will always decide, "What's in it for me?" Since we all ask this question, we set ourselves up for people who provide persuasive answers. What's in it for producers is getting their products sold. Create a want. Make it feel like a need. Everybody else is buying it. Without it you will feel deprived. God, however, does not have a consumer mentality. It's good for us to know that when we pray. No amount of hype is going to manipulate our God. God knows what we need before we ask. God does not have Big Mac attacks.

Someone with a consumer mentality will not put out money on something without being convinced it's worth the price. Sometimes the consumer knows it isn't worth the price as a product, but they're willing to pay in order to have something "everybody else" thinks it's important to have. They are willing to pay for prestige. Someone with a consumer mentality will become a victim of fads. I remember a female professor, for instance, who always dressed the same. Some people thought she was a nun because she always wore the same blue business suits. She laughed and said, "I come into style every few years."

God does not fall for fads. God looked on human beings and saw brokenness, imperfection, sinfulness, and terminal fallenness. So God sent his only-begotten Son to pay the highest price to mend it all. Those of us with a consumer mentality will find this transaction of God totally amazing. May our amazement lead us to praise and thanksgiving!

O God of Promise,
    it is so easy to see the world around me
    as a flat reality of one dimension.
My home, my car, my clothes
    can appear simply as material things
    which I buy and sell, use and discard.
The people with whom I work and play
    can seem as mere agents of production or pleasure
    who contribute to my wealth or leisure.
Let me see every material possession
    as a gift from your hand.
Let me recognize every person I encounter
    as your child, bound for glory.
Amen.

The Hazards of Hypocrisy

Can you imagine anything more unlikely than asking a child what he or she wants to be when grown up and getting the answer: "I want to be a hypocrite"? No one wants to be a hypocrite. One would think that any attempt to avoid hypocrisy deserves applause but, actually, there are many hazards. Some of them can leave us clear of hypocrisy, but scarred in another way. In a laudable search for authenticity, one could subscribe to an adage, such as "Honesty is the best policy," and really clobber somebody.

"What do you think of my new dress? I bought it just for you!"

"I think it makes you uglier than you truly are."

No hypocrisy there, all right! But our best instincts tell us something good and holy has been violated. Without too much reflection, we probably realize it was the law of love. Jesus told us the greatest of all virtues is charity, not honesty. I remember a high school retreat when the retreat master said something to this effect: "Hypocrisy is being other than you are for an unworthy motive; but being other than you are for a worthy motive is conversion."

Gracious God, help us to be the authentic persons you have called us to be without leaving victims in our wake.

Jesus, Son of David,
   have pity on me!
You are the light that heals all blindness.
You are the love that feeds all longing.
You are the grace that allow hearts
   to believe again and again.
Help me to see your will for me.
Help me to see you, to serve you
   in the alienated and the poor.
Help me to profess you in what I say,
      and in what I do
   that others may come to know and love you.
Jesus, Son of David,
      help me to be the person
   you have called me to be.
Amen.

Out of Egypt

When the Hebrew people experienced the power of the God of Moses, they asked: "Is there really a God of compassion who considers us valuable and delights in rescuing us, forgiving us, and showering us with gifts of life and love and land? How is this God unlike the gods of our pagan neighbors? Has this God of ours shown similar compassion to anyone else we know? What will this great God of ours do next?" As they addressed the questions, we received the stories of Abraham, Isaac, Jacob, and Noah, and the creation stories of Genesis.

This is the way it worked for them and it's the way it works for us. We do not live history, we make history. In the Bible, we read about creation, then the Fall, punishment, and redemption. That's right! And then redemption happened. Then people became aware of all the rest of the story. Isn't this our experience too? Someone becomes a millionaire in the lottery and only then do we ask who they are, where they came from, what they did. Redemption comes first, not last.

Think about falling in love. When it happens, almost magically, suddenly there are so many new questions about the beloved, questions that didn't make any difference before. Maybe this is the way it is in the kingdom Jesus proclaimed. Maybe we need an experience of its joy, peace, justice, mercy, and harmony. Such an experience is a kind of redemption. And we can do this for one another, too, can't we? We have the power to bring someone out of Egypt with our kindness.

*L*ord Jesus,
>you come to me as living bread,
>given up for the life of the world.
Like Elijah in the desert,
>may I eat and drink
>>of the spiritual nourishment
>>that you offer me.
You brought your covenant people
>from the hardships of the desert
>>to the redemption of your promised land.
May I always recognize the presence
>of your love in my life
>>and share the experience
>of your peace and harmony.
Amen.

Staying in Fashion Isn't Easy

There was a time when the only clothes with labels on the outside were overalls (Oshkosh, b'gosh) and jeans. Now brand names are blaring from every piece of clothing. Now there are sweats for every season. Halloween, Christmas, Valentine's Day. If you want to show off your patriotism you have sweaters, jackets, and dresses that feature the American flag. As much as we Americans like to think of ourselves as rugged individualists, the quality of our conformity is hilarious. Instead of shaping our own destiny and identity, we are being shaped by a power outside ourselves. Often, we are not even aware of this power, and its effectiveness lies in its innocence and anonymity.

We hear Jesus calling the apostles in the liturgy, "Come, follow me." They leave their nets and start a spiritual journey marked by sporadic fidelity. Trying to make the agenda of Jesus their own, they often fall into the power of the fashion of their day and think of the kingdom of God as a temporal sway of might, more powerful than the Romans.

Confronted by the Scriptures we encounter, perhaps we might take a look at the powers which tend to shape our lives. As we take an honest look at ourselves, can we assert that Jesus' agenda—to realize the kingdom of God—is our agenda? If not, are we going to take charge of our lives or simply flow with the fashion?

*L*ord Jesus,
Sometimes it is easier to go along
 than to challenge the status quo.
Sometimes it is more simple to suffer indignity
 than to rock the boat.
Sometimes it seems safer to bite my lip
 than to call the question.
I know that your Gospel calls me to love and forgive,
 to humble myself and to take up my cross.
Give me the strength to oppose what is wrong
 in words that are bold and clear.
Grant me the courage to stand for the truth
 not only in love but also in strength.
Amen.

A Story Worth Telling!

Drought-stricken farmers in South Carolina were being forced to sell their dairy cattle because they had no feed. With the plentiful rain that spring, hay crops were very good in Indiana and other Midwest states. So many Midwest farmers donated hay to the dairy farmers in South Carolina. They had something to give and they came through.

With farm prices being what they are, most farmers are desperate financially. Had they been asked to give money, it might have been tough, but I suspect they would have tried.

I once served as a country pastor in a small town. No post office, no buildings, just a church and cornfields. There were about forty families in the parish, all farmers. Our church was twice as big as it needed to be, and we only had one Mass on Sunday. Everybody came, children and all. They sat in the last half of the church, except for one family, which always took the second pew on Saint Joseph's side.

One day, I decided that we needed to install a new tile floor. I did the vestibule myself, so the parishioners could see how it improved the looks of the floor. When I asked the men to show up Wednesday afternoon to get the whole job done, I was not surprised when one man called to say he couldn't make it. What surprised me was that all the rest came, ready to work. I had to go buy more beer! So I pay tribute to farmers and their witness of giving—it always impresses me when I see the needy giving.

*T*he majesty of your hand
    and the splendor of your voice,
        O God of heaven and earth,
    have touched our little world
        and have lifted us from darkness.
Instill in us a spirit of servant generosity,
        revealed in the life of your Son,
    who did not seek earthly power,
        but who gave his life on our behalf.
Draw us into the circle of this heavenly love,
    which lasts forever and ever.
Amen.

The Table Versus the TV Tray

In Confirmation interviews I always ask, "What's your favorite food?" No one ever mentions food they eat at home. How to interpret this is beyond me, but I suspect it's because people have so much to do that it's hard to have a family meal.

I had the privilege of hearing a Methodist minister expound a theology of table that was very scriptural and provocative. He took off on our culture and rather convincingly showed how we have lost our sense of intimacy, promoted an isolated individualism, and disconnected ourselves from one another because we simply don't sit down and feast together very much. The TV dinner has become a powerful symbol of this change in our culture.

His stories of the many times significant moments in Jesus' ministry that happened at meals were very enlightening. Cana, Zacchaeus, Mary Magdalene, the Pharisee who invited Jesus to dinner, and the Last Supper. Jesus was carrying on a Hebrew tradition of hospitality but, true to form, he added his own twist. Hebrews felt obligated to feed any one who came through their camp. However, they did not allow enemies to eat with them. Jesus ate with enemies, including Judas, who betrayed him.

He concluded with the scriptural image of the messianic banquet, which will happen when the kingdom has come. I have always known that Christians are called to be countercultural, but never before did I realize that it all starts with family dinner. Bon appetit!

*T*aste and see the goodness of the Lord,
    for God has given his very flesh and blood.
        We are nourished and strengthened.
Our spirits are parched and dry and you say,
    "Come to the table I have set before you."
        The wine of your blood quenches our thirst
        and refreshes our spirits.
Our soul is weakened by the evil of our day
    and the foolishness of our choices.
        You say, "Come eat of my flesh
        which is life for eternity."
The flesh of your body replenishes our strength
    and fills us to overflowing
        with your Spirit of truth.
We give thanks and we bless you, Lord.
Amen.

Hostility Absorber

When the lease was up on a vehicle I used to drive, I could tell it was about that time because the shock absorbers were rather worn. It just couldn't take the bumps the way it could when the shock absorbers were new. Bumps occur many places besides on the road. People bump into each other a lot. Some have good shock absorbers for others' hostility, and some do not.

Those who have poor quality hostility absorbers react by attacking back, defending self, calling people names, or sometimes making nasty signs. The funny thing is, each of us needs to get rid of hostility somehow. Often we use those closest to us—whose love we do not doubt—as our victims. But it works both ways. One day the victim, the next day the aggressor.

So to accept another's hostility without fighting back is a real service. And it's Christian. Jesus showed us how to be a hostility absorber. And it cost him his life. Normally our life is not at stake because we are not asked to carry the hostility of all humankind—just the passing aggression of someone with a claim on our love. Fight it, and it gets worse. Accept it, and it gets healed.

*B*lessed are you, Shepherd God,
  for the wonderful way you care for me
  when I am in need.
Blessed are you, good and faithful Shepherd,
  for the still more marvelous way
  you ask me to care for my sisters and brothers
    when they are in need.
May I be, like you,
  a loving friend to those
  who are touched by my life.
May I be, like you,
  willing to give myself to them in love,
  caring for them and never reacting in kind
    to hostility or anger.
Amen.

Dabitur Vobis

When Jesus was about to send the disciples out on a preaching mission very early in their ministry training, they asked him: "But what are we to say?" He answered: "It shall be given to you." (In Latin, *dabitur vobis.*) One weekend, after six wonderful days of vacation, I came back feeling unprepared and uninspired. Although I had a homily all written out, it didn't do a thing for me. I was feeling sorry that my vacation had been short and was now over.

But I preached anyway, and was not happy with myself. A funny thing happened. I got more compliments on that homily that I was ashamed of than I had ever gotten before! Now figure that one out, if you can. My analysis is that Jesus continues, through the Holy Spirit, to do what he promised those disciples: the *dabitur vobis* thing.

But sometimes the "you" in the "It shall be given to you" is not the preacher, but the people. They are somehow given an openness to hear powerful messages sent through weak words. Just as on Pentecost, the Holy Spirit moved the people to hear Peter. They heard him not because he was so eloquent or accomplished as a public speaker (he was just a fisherman), but because their hearts were opened. They even heard him in their own language, although he was speaking in his native Aramaic dialect.

Something like that happened that weekend at Saint Elizabeth Seton, I suspect.

Come, dwell in us,
    Father, Son, and Spirit.
Your works of creation,
    salvation, and sanctification
    are trustworthy and true.
Your mouth spoke but a word
    and all was created
    and it is good.
Your breath is the breath of the Spirit
    that makes all things whole and worthy.
Your heart became flesh,
    dwelling in our midst
       to save and set us free.
What can we offer in return
    for your blessed kindness?
Only to listen to your Word
    and fill our whole being with your breath
       poured out in love.
Amen.